FIRST FLOOR
ROOM 16

Hilarious Confessions of a Male Escort in London
A Real Story

Maximo Kovak

For more information:
www.maximokovak.com

First Edition, 2013
ISBN: 978-0-9575953-0-9

Disclaimer:
The author, who decided to keep himself anonymous, portrays his experiences as a male escort whilst living in London. All the names and locations have been changed to make sure real characters in the book won't be recognised.

Any resemblance to any person is purely coincidental, although some aspects of the characters may have been inspired by some persons I actually know and admire.

Cover: The model on the cover is not an escort or the author. The author holds the rights for the use of that image.

Book design by Maureen Cutajar
www.gopublished.com

Dedicated to my friend Jonny,

Who calls himself a cum slut.

He is an honest, cocksure and funny good friend.

Thanks for motivating me to write this book.

‘I am just a musical prostitute, my dear.’
Freddie Mercury

INTRODUCTION

The story in this book is real.

The author, who decided to keep himself anonymous, portrays his experiences as a male escort whilst living in London. All the names and locations have been changed to make sure real characters in the book won't be recognised.

The book enters the alleys of male prostitution, describing true situations and funny anecdotes that happened to the author while escorting.

The book reveals two characters, Pablo and Pedro, whose stories unfold in parallel, giving the reader an inside out on the lives of the escort (Pedro) and the person (Pablo).

The hilarious sexual adventures will enlighten you about today's gay sexuality, appealing to both straight and gay readers, male or female.

A handy dictionary describing some of the sexual terms and abbreviations appearing here in has been added by the author at the end of the book.

If you wish to contact or ask any questions to the author, you can speak directly to him using the blog and comments section in the website created for this book: maximokovak.com

By the way, the sexy guy appearing on the book cover is not an escort or the author.

CHAPTER 1

BUT YOU ARE NOT BLACK

When you do this job you have to be prepared for all sorts of situations and follow your intuition to get out of trouble fast.

I received these messages online from a profile called Blktop29:

Blktop29 – *"Hi Pedro, I would like to arrange a meeting with you today. Are you versatile? Are you into Black guys? I am into rough safe play. I'm quite dominant in bed. Is that your scene? How much for you to come to my place at 1 pm today? Adam"*

Pedro – *"Hi Adam, Yes I am versatile and I can take rough play. Have to be safe though. I had many black clients before; ethnicities are not an issue for me. Send me a sms text on my mobile now with the full address and postcode and I will meet you there at 1 pm."*

Blktop29 – *"I am happy to pass you my mobile but I have to be discreet so I would prefer to meet you outside the tube station next to my house. I will pick you up there at 1 pm and bring you to my place. Is that ok?"*

Rule number 1 for an escort: Never travel to meet a client without having his contact number. If something happens, you won't have any proof or way to contact the client. Many people make fake bookings and once you arrive at the place they don't appear or you realise that the address is false. That is essential, especially if you are not meeting at his house or hotel. I never travel without having an address but it's not every day I get a message from a super sexy black guy, top, well endowed and into rough safe play. Almost impossible! I decided to play it cool and be flexible this time.

Pedro – "*That is ok Adam. Send me a text sms message now so I have your number and I will meet you outside the station at 1 pm. Will text you when I arrive. Pedro ;)*"

The routine of getting ready for an out-call was more elaborate than usual this time. I wanted to create a very good impression and look my best. The client sent the text message as requested so I was able to save his number. The way he spoke and approached me indicated a well educated person, direct and clear about what he wants. Probably not the first time meeting an escort, and most possibly a business man or a guy with a busy life and partnered.

I decided to wear smart-casual clothes, nice trousers and a shirt. Nothing over the top, but nicely presented none the less. I packed into my leather suitcase all the escort tools for the session: lube, condoms, massage oil, a couple of dildos in case he likes that and poppers.

I arrived five minutes before at the tube station and I texted him to let him know I was waiting outside. He replied saying that he would meet me in five minutes. I sent a message describing the type of clothes I was wearing, so it was easier for him to identify me.

A very nice sports car arrived and parked on the other side of the road three minutes after, the type of car that boys use to impress girls. Will that be my client? I could not see the driver clearly from a distance but the horn started to pip-pip and I commenced to move towards the car. When I was next to it the driver opened the door, so obviously it was me he was pipping at. I got into the car and smiled.

"How are you doing?" I asked.

"I am great thanks, were you waiting long?"

"No, just a couple of minutes."

The driver was a very smart, hunky and super sexy white English guy. He had a beautiful face, blue eyes, rugby player legs and with such a body, obviously a gym membership. I did not have time to say anything else; the guy was already driving fast around the neighbourhood.

I tried to keep calm while hundreds of thoughts ran through my head in seconds.

But my client is black, who is this guy? Did he lie and show false profile photos? Did my client send a friend to pick me up? Does my client have in mind to have a threesome with me and this guy but he did not mention it?

"So is the house far away?"

"The house is very close" he said. "But we are going to stop at the office first."

At the office! What the hell is going on here? My heart started to pump faster and I was finding it difficult to keep a calm face. I decided to be a bit more direct.

"Listen, don't take it wrongly, but I am a bit disappointed."

"What do you mean?"

"Well, you are not black!"

The driver looked at me confused and gave me a frown. "Well, we have a black guy working in the office."

"Your profile photos are of a black man. I don't understand why you put false photos in it?"

Suddenly we got immersed in a silence of several seconds that seemed to be for years. The car stopped at a gate entrance and the driver turned and looked at me. "Were you waiting for another agent at the station by any chance?"

I was shocked when I heard that. I had to keep calm, and think. All was becoming clear now. This guy was supposed to be picking up a client and show him some houses on sale. That is why he wants to go to the office first! He thought I was his client as I was waiting in the same spot where he was supposed to meet him. I was wearing smart clothes and had a nice leather suitcase, so I could perfectly well be a business man wanting to buy a house in the area. Ohhh shit, what a mess! Where is my client then? He must be waiting at the station by now. Ok, compose yourself, calm down.

"I am afraid yes; I was waiting for another agent. This must be a terrible confusion, sorry."

"Well, I guess the best thing to do is to take you back to the station" he said.

I nodded my head approvingly and the car started to move fast through the streets. We did not speak whilst he was driving back. I guess we were both shocked about the situation but I was the only one who knew the whole truth behind all the confusion, or I hoped so.

The car arrived at the station and we both saw a white guy and a black guy standing outside. We got out of the car and approached our guys; the black guy was for me and the white guy for the agent. We looked at each other for a second with a half smile and a complicity gaze while shaking hands with our respective man. This time it was the right one.

I guess you now want to know all the intimate details of what happened with the client afterwards, don't you?

Well, I will tell you one thing only: It was amazing!

CHAPTER 2

DUALISM

Since I started escorting, my life and my sexuality split into two. I am Pedro the escort, and Pablo the person. Both characters feed into each other and coexist together.

Pedro brings the money and Pablo spends it and takes decisions.

Pedro is a dominant rough top in bed and Pablo is a submissive naughty bottom.

Pablo influences Pedro's sexual activities by adding new techniques, styles or sexual games that he learnt with his lovers, and Pedro uses it with his clients. Pablo is very organised, creative and charming so Pedro absorbs these qualities and uses it in his work.

Pedro has his own mobile phone and clothes for business and Pablo has his for personal, pleasure or everyday work.

Many escorts learn to live with this dualism or bipolarity but for some guys the fine line between these two characters can be confusing and create conflicts.

My way to deal with this is to make sure that Pablo keeps his feet on the floor doing projects, others activities or some extra work apart from escorting. The contact with 'normal' people and real life keeps Pedro under control.

I have been doing this job for five years now and I learned many things from it. I have a better understanding about how sexuality works and about people. I met very interesting VIP clients that I would never have met with other types of jobs. I have travelled all around the world visiting clients and have been able to contrast different cultures and their approaches to life and sexuality.

I became a 'sexual fantasies provider'. People contact me and explain to me what they want, from a cuddle session and sensual body contact with massage to kinky complex sessions where the darkest fantasies are fulfilled. My job is to provide that for them all.

Some people find it difficult to understand why a guy like me with university studies and quite a lot of work experience keeps doing an escort job. I guess this job gives me the freedom that other jobs won't be able to provide, and for me it is like having a rest after many years of studies and working really hard in other jobs.

I know this won't last forever but while it does I am enjoying it as much as I can.

Wouldn't you, if you could?

CHAPTER 3

TYPES OF ESCORTS

The English language always manages to soften terms that sound offensive or discriminatory and change it for others which are more appealing by using euphemisms. For example the terms 'prostitute', 'whore' or 'rent boy' have been exchanged for the term 'escort'.

Definitions for Escort in the Oxford Dictionary:

A group of persons, or a single person, accompanying another or others for protection, guidance, or courtesy: An escort of sailors accompanied the queen.

A person, specially a man, who takes somebody to a particular social event.

A person, specially a woman who is paid to go out socially.

We know that prostitutes can be female, male or transgender. I am a male escort so I will concentrate on that group.

But what are the types of male escorts? Are they all the same?

Based on what I have seen I will divide them into different groups:

The casual escorts: Mostly students in need of cash, people that lost their jobs or guys with some financial problem that needs to be solved urgently. They try escorting for a short time to get the extra cash needed or they do it on and off for short periods. Mostly students in their early twenties with not much experience in the field, and therefore with a big possibility to make mistakes, depending on their desperation for money. There are a small percentage of casual escorts that are not students or people with financial problems, but have normal jobs. They do escorting in their free time for extra cash or for other reasons. Casual escorts are very worried about being recognised so they normally advertise hiding their faces to avoid friends or relatives recognising them.

The full time escorts: For them escorting is not only their main job but also their lifestyle. In this group there are experienced guys that take their job seriously; they know how to trade, where to advertise and how to deal with clients. But you can also find guys that have lost their focus; they got involved with drugs or become depressed and their lives go in a negative circle from which they can't escape.

Most full time escorts advertise their faces (unless they are plain ugly) as they know they can get more clientele that way and they are used to being recognised in the gay scene.

The VIP escorts: There is no such thing as a full time VIP male escort who exclusively meets very rich and important clients all the time. Some special escorts are able and prepared to deal with this type of client.

To become a VIP escort does not depend entirely on the escort but also on the VIP client who has chosen him. To enter this category the escort should have some of these characteristics: guys that look smart, are educated and with good manners, able to speak at least two languages, very well organised and knowledgeable about protocol and etiquette for social events. They know what to wear for each occasion or event, they are able to sit with their client and other guests at a dinner party and chat with ambassadors, business men and even royalty, never embarrassing their client. They are good at sex. They don't have passport restrictions to travel to any country.

By having some of these characteristics they might be able to attract some VIP clients and they could become their regulars for a while. VIP clients normally test the escort for small events first, and if he passes the test, behaves and satisfies the client, then he may become a regular and will bring him to more important social events. Most VIP escorts are also full time escorts, otherwise they won't be able to have flexibility to travel abroad to meet their VIP clients.

There are also some very exclusive agencies connected to model agencies that sometimes provide exclusive VIP service for very wealthy clients. The agencies propose to some of their models the extra job and if they accept they enter to form part of their elite portfolio. These models travel all around the world to meet super rich clients for company and intimate service, getting paid ridiculous amounts of money. These agencies do not advertise and everything is done discreetly and based in high profile networking.

You will probably be asking yourself, what type of escort is Pedro?

Well, I started as a casual escort when I was in my last year at university in the UK. I was doing a BA in Filmmaking and Video production. I had two 'normal' part time jobs at the time and I was also full time at uni. I was paying for my studies and I was struggling financially in my last year, as the final project was expensive. I wanted to do a good project and get top marks so I needed to find a solution to bring cash fast, without taking much more time from my studies or interfering with my other jobs.

To escort or not to escort, that was the question.

I am not Shakespeare, but I asked myself this question the first time I considered doing the job. The escort option seemed to be more practical to sort out the problem so I tried and it worked out, then I became a full time escort when I moved to London after uni.

I spent many months applying for jobs related to my degree, video production, however my age and low practical experience did not help much. I did a lot of research and applied to hundreds of places but I did not get a single response. I was devastated to see that my three years at uni did not help one iota to get a normal job in the field, so I decided to continue doing escorting to survive in London while I was deciding plan number two.

While working as a full time escort, I realised that this job could be very profitable if I treated it as a real job, like someone that goes every day to the office.

I always have been a very focused and organised person so it was not difficult for me to be successful as an escort. With time I started to meet some VIP clients.

I eventually became a VIP escort and travelled all around the world to meet high profile clients for short periods, and be with them in events as a companion. Dubai, Nairobi, Chennai, Geneva, Oslo, Paris, Athens, Cairo, Kuwait, Istanbul and Berlin are just some of the cities I have visited to meet clients.

So during all this process I have been all three types of escort. Some guys think that by putting 'VIP escort' in their profiles they will attract more clients or rich clients, but things do not work that way. Others which have done porn movies decide to put 'Porn star' in their profiles, thinking this will boost up their business. Some clients might get turned on by the fact they have done porn and book them. Many others will laugh at it and take it as an arrogant remark and probably be put off by it.

You will never see such descriptions in my profiles or adverts. I prefer to let my clients decide what I am once they meet me.

At the beginning I used to meet escorts for fun and curiosity. I wanted to know more about them. I saw so many nasty and sad situations so I decided to keep myself apart and now I only meet escorts for duos or professionals encounters.

Don't misunderstand me, I don't have anything against other guys doing the same job, but I realised that to keep balanced and do this job I need a certain normality in my life, and mixing with escorts wouldn't bring me such peace but more temptations and drama.

I will never forget one of the first escorts I met in London when I was starting. Anthony was a young English lad in his early twenties who contacted me through my profile wanting to meet for fun. We arranged a meeting at his place in central London. I liked his photos and he played the type of sex I was looking for, so I said yes. When I met him he looked very different to his pictures. He looked older in person and was extremely skinny. I noticed he was kind of high on some drug as he was speaking very slowly and with long pauses in between sentences. His flat, in spite of being an expensive flat, looked like a tramp shelter. Everything was extremely dirty and messy and I had to wade through clothes, magazines, papers and beer cans while moving around. The bathroom and the main bedroom were in no better condition. I could not understand how he could entertain clients there, but I did not want to be rude or impolite with him, so I didn't make any comments.

I wanted to know more about him. He was a lovely guy but he seemed lonely and let himself fall in to the dark side of drugs, party life and decadence. He asked me about my life and when I explained that I was finishing the last year of my degree and that I was planning to move to London soon, he tried to impress me telling me about a couple of small courses that he did and other things that he was willing to achieve but obviously we both knew that it wouldn't happen if he continued the type of life he was following. We had sex and it was good but I felt uncomfortable to see him in such state. He took some drugs while I was there so he got even higher.

For me, meeting this guy was an eye opener. I now knew what mistakes I should not make when I moved to London.

My second encounter wasn't great either, but definitely another eye opener.

I met Anthony again and we went for lunch. I didn't know much about London or the escort life there so decided to meet him again. After lunch he asked me to go with him to meet some friends in the Earls Court area. Me, the innocent boy, said yes and had no idea about what was coming.

We arrived outside a house in Earls Court. He rang the bell and suddenly two high-pitched queens starting shouting through one window in a top flat. "He's here! He's here! Hello darling! Oooh, who is that handsome boy that you have with you?"

We entered the small hall of a flat and a group of very camp and feminine guys starting to cuddle and kiss Anthony. They all looked at me and I shook hands with them in a manly fashion and introduced myself. We entered one room that was supposed to be the lounge where a couple of guys were on laptops checking their profiles and using chat rooms.

I deduced that they were escorts too. Most of them were English but I noticed two of them had foreign accents. There were four camp boys and two transsexuals there. I was a bit shocked with the situation so I decided to keep a low profile and observe.

The guys were chatting not stop to Anthony, asking questions and gossiping about some friends and other escorts in a funny way. Smiles, laughs and loud comments followed. Some of them asked me questions and I answered while smiling.

Suddenly the door bell rang several times. All the boys got jumpy and started to move around the room speaking to each other. One of the trannys left the room and I could hear her saying, "Yes, come up!"

The boys became silent as I heard the main door opening and the tranny speaking with a man behind our door. Two minutes later the tranny re-entered the lounge. “Come on girls, we need to parade!”

Everyone got together in a queue except me. My eyes were wide open observing the situation.

“Come on boy, get in the queue!” said the tranny while looking at me-

Somewhat surprised, I joined the end of the queue.

They started moving towards the hall and entered the next room. We were in a one bedroom Victorian flat. The door opened and I saw a man sat on a large bed looking at us. He was in his late 40s, a bit chunky and had quite a serious face.

The tranny next to the man introduced us one by one using our nick-names. Each one passed in front of the man and then left the room to go back to the lounge. I don’t remember my facial expression when passing the man but I can assure you that it was good enough for a framed picture.

We were all in the lounge again in silence when the tranny suddenly entered the lounge. “The winner is Jonathan!” he said while smiling and making wrist flapping poses by the door.

Jonathan, a twink in his 20s, blond hair, a bit overweigh and quite camp, left the room and went to meet the man.

It was only then that I realised where I was and what was going on. I was in an improvised and impoverished brothel.

I looked at Anthony and he smiled at me, knowing that I understood.

I had a few more encounters with other escorts after that:

Shine, the Thai-Asian escort who introduced me to the pleasures of fisting and ass play. He was in his late thirties but looked twenty-nine and had a very handsome and smooth body. A lovely guy but again, affected by the heavy drugs and the hard life style. His moods changed like the wind and I could not cope with his emotional explosions.

Tony, an English escort aged thirty-eight who was a gentleman and had very good manners, but trapped in the Tina (Crystal Meth) substance too. After seeing him in very sad situations where he degraded his own dignity, I decided it was time to stop meeting him.

Jarek, the Czech escort. He had a great sense of humour, was very healthy and mature guy for a 22years old. We became good friends for a while.

Jaro, the twenty-five year old Black English escort. A casual escort living with his parents, studying at uni, with a part time 'normal' job and a boyfriend. He was a smart guy, excellent manners, very sexy and masculine, tall and hunky. We had the greatest sex together and I liked him personally. I had a crush on him but he was already spoken for so it was not possible to establish anything serious at that time.

☧ ☧ ☧

The escort life is good on the one hand as you manage your own time. You are self-employed and it is quite profitable. However as any freelance might know, you have to be quite disciplined and look after your clients otherwise they won't come back. Escorts have to live with seasonal ups and downs, times where you can earn lot of money and other times when you don't have any clients at all. Money management skills are essential to be successful in this job and survive. Many escorts fail on that and get into trouble.

The psychological pressure of the job brings escorts down often, and during low times or depression it is very easy to make mistakes. I tackle that by keeping one foot on the ground, by living with normal people with normal jobs rather than with other escorts. Doing other activities and jobs always helps too.

Today I went to the supermarket and whilst I was waiting in

the queue to pay, I observed the guy working at the till. He was around twenty-five years old, white, and average looking but energetic. He was doing his job mechanically but by his way of chatting with the customers and the look in his eyes I could not help to think that guy wanted more in his life and he was a bit fed up.

He seemed to be ambitious and not stupid at all, however he was there doing that job.

I smiled at him and he said good morning while starting to scan my items. I was wearing smart clothes, a nice shirt and trousers and was holding my Iphone on my hand. I noticed he was observing me too, looking at me while doing his job.

"Working today or day off?" he asked me suddenly.

If I had told him that I was off, he wouldn't have understood why I was wearing smart office clothes on a Saturday and also he would feel bad as he was there totally bored scanning product after product all day.

"I am actually working today" I replied with a smile.

"Do you mind me asking what do you do?"

I was a bit shocked about his personal approach but I decided to be friendly. "I work in video production."

"Oh, do you do films?"

I answered yes by nodding my head. The conversation finished there and I smiled again when taking the receipt and leaving.

My intuition didn't fail, he wanted more in his life and he was probably asking himself; why can I not be like this guy? Of course he does not know my real story but he made his prejudgments based on what he saw in that moment.

On my way back home I could not help but feel happy and also guilty. I am very fortunate to be able to do my escort job and earn good money, and also have so much free time, but I felt guilty seeing that guy earning probably £6 per hour, working hard.

Those thoughts brought me back to my university days when I spent three years working hard in two part times jobs earning as much as the cashier I just met in the supermarket. During my last year at uni I continued doing those jobs but I also was earning £100 per hour doing the escort job. I remember going to my normal jobs, working with my colleagues and thinking "what would they say or think if they knew that I also have an extra job where I earn in one hour what they earn in three days?"; that taught me to respect people who do normal jobs and keep my feet on the ground.

☧ ☧ ☧

Speaking about types of escorts, have you ever read escort profiles? Well, you might find all sorts of contents depending on the escort. Here are some real examples [sic]:

The ego ones: *"Best escort in town. Porn star and VIP escort. You won't forget a night with me. Pure muscle for your satisfaction and waiting to be worshiped. Call now."*

The sexual ones: *"Hi Guys. A hot/horny/hung Danish/English guy, give the most amazing massage. Imagine this: you lying on the bed, I'm sitting across you just wearing small white briefs. I start on your shoulders, working down your back, massaging the oil into your back, relaxing your muscles. Then I start with my fingers, working them over your neck, down your back and over your arse... While you moan.... Or... You walk in, get pushed against the wall... stripped and patted down. Tied up on the bed-frame, blindfolded, abused, spanked, made to worship my big cock, spat on, pissed on and when you think you have tried most stuff, you will feel my hard cock press against your hungry hole."*

The lazy ones: *"Ask / call."*

The confusing ones: *"Sublime would be if all people we knew and we didn't need an education! But then we would have no motivation to learn, because we would know who is who ... Thus becoming a living monotone, where there is no advantage to anyone! I am sure that we spend a great time, I am able to show you some ways you might not know about..."*

The reassuring ones: *"PICTURES WITH NO PHOTOSHOP!!! Hey there! Easy going guy here, very straight acting, into most things... With a good sense of humour, I have an open and friendly personality, Smart, University educated, fun and sophisticated. I'm professional, always offer a good service, respect people and expect the same in return. THOSE ARE MY REAL PHOTOS, NO AIR-BRUSH, NO PHOTOSHOP, NO TRICKS. WHAT YOU SEE IS WHAT YOU GET."*

The rhetoric ones: *"Nando is the guy next door type, full of life, loves having fun and lives a playboy lifestyle and that is why he left his parents' home to have a free life and works as an escort and model. He is very open minded, intelligent and educated and does not miss classes at Uni. He does not like talking about how he looks but lets the pics do the talking. He is discreet as many bisexuals are in his pics but each part of that body is real. He is versatile, with genuine 9 inches and a body to take your breath away, his favourite part of the body is the eyes, which are penetrating. His killer smile can light a whole town. If you are looking for fun, love, vibes with a modern and refined guy, Nando is for you. On that private moment Nando can be hot and spicy. He can be a great dominant or a sexy romantic lover making your wishes become true."*

The shocking ones: *"IM NOT GOING TO GIVE THE REGULAR BULSH*T OF HOW SMART, INTELLIGENT, WISE, OR OTHER SH*T ALL THE OTHER HOOKERS GIVE YOU! THAT YOU*

WILL DISCOVER BY YOUR SELF ONCE YOU MEET ME.
CUT TO THE CHASE! I F U C K LIKE A BEAST! I AM NOT A PROSTITUTE!
I DO NOT WORK FOR YOU.
YOUR MONEY IS YOUR WAY TO MAKE YOUR WISHES COME TRUE! NOT A WAY TO BUY ME!
ARE WE CLEAR?"

The standard ones: *"My name is Tom and I'm a very horny British guy. I also have an advanced diploma in body massage. I'm reliable, friendly, always horny and ready to please.*

Come see me in my luxury flat in Soho Central London, just minutes away from Tottenham Court Road and Leicester Square tube stations. Or let me come see you.

SERIOUS INQUIRES ONLY. CALL NOW"

As you can see there is a big variety of descriptions and types of adverts, my advert is standard but direct and I use certain types of keywords that I know will attract the kind of clients I am looking for.

The escort profiles and adverts are the main tools for the sex workers to attract their clientele.

What you write there or the type of photos you disclosed will influence the type of people you get.

For example, I know that my Mediterranean masculine look attracts mostly bottom clients looking for the macho Hispanic or Arab type, for that reason I focus my adverts on that idea. I have clear face, body and cock pictures on my profile and I selected a series of photos examples with kinky sexual activities I play, to enhance the client's imagination. I did not want to lose the top clients so I also left a couple of sexy bum shots but not more, otherwise I will put off the bottom clients.

90% of my clientele are bottoms or submissive guys and 10% tops.

My profile text is clear, direct and informative but also open to options:

"NOT ALWAYSIN FRONT OF COMPUTER ...CALL TO CONTACT ME

SAFE SEX ONLY ...DO NOT ASK FOR BAREBACK

SPANISH VERSATILE GUY 8 ". I am very masculine. "Relax and Discretion guaranteed"

I PLAY ALL SORT OF SEX SCENES INCLUDING EXTREME AND VERY ROUGH, ASK FOR DETAILS

IN CALL AT MY PLACE

OUT CALL AT YOUR HOTEL OR HOUSE

OVERNIGHTS

WEEKENDS

DUOS / GROUPS

CAN TRAVEL NATIONALLY AND INTERNATIONALLY FOR SHORT PERIODS."

I take my escort job as a profession. I do my own accounts about expenditures and dedicate many hours in front of my computer chatting with clients and arranging bookings.

In a single month an escort could spend anything from £300 to £700 in advertisement and escort tools.

Magazine advert £120 per month

Online profiles £60 each, per month (some escorts have two or three)

Special lube, toys sterilisers, poppers, sex toys, massage oil etc £80 per month

Taxis to meet clients late night about £200 per month

Candles and incenses £20 per month

Every escort earns different amounts per month depending how successful they are and also depending the seasons. But the average amount per month is anything between £1.500 and £5000 in good months.

I have found some escorts who are organised and manage their money very well but others can be a disaster and they are always getting into trouble or short of cash. When you get such amounts of money very quickly many guys get a bit extravagant with their spending and waste their money on stupid things without thinking of the future or saving for bad months.

To have people that treat you like a sex object or perceive you as a sex god can sometimes be flattering but also very annoying. I have had people pointing at me or whispering to friends when they see me in the gay scene. You get used to that but sometimes it upsets me as they are judging me for what they see or superficially know about me. The worst part comes when you are in social events or parties with other friends that don't do the job and people start asking you what you do for a living. At those times I would love to say I am a prostitute and see the reaction of people trying to hide their shock but you don't want to embarrass your friends or create any drama so I finish saying any other thing related to my other work.

To do escorting does not create any personal conflict for me but it is just a transition time whilst I get back to being Pablo 100%.

CHAPTER 4

THE BEGINNING 1975

In 1975 I was just four years old but I remember images floating in my mind of two very important events. One shaped my life and the other changed my whole country.

The first one was the separation of my parents. I have this image in my mind in slow motion of me holding my auntie's hand. She was taking me back home after a trip to the park with her baby son. When we got out of the lift on the fourth floor, we saw my father shouting and banging our door violently. "Open the door immediately. Who do you think you are, bitch! This is my house and I am the man, how you dare to lock me out! Open it or I will kill you!"

Next to my father we saw two suitcases. My aunty approached my father after pushing me behind her to protect me.

"Pablo, get behind me" she said.

"What is happening Antonio?" she said to my father, "Calm down please, the neighbours are going to notice the shouting."

What I remember next is that I was living at my grandmother's house. My mother moved there after the separation.

When I was older my family explained to me that my mother had suffered domestic violence and she had coped with the situation for several years until the violence also started towards my older brothers and sister. The line was crossed and one day when my father was away, she changed the door lock and put my father's belongings into two suitcases and left them outside.

I do not remember anything before the day mother threw him out but my brothers and sister do.

I realise now how much courage my mother had to have to do what she did. She did not have the opportunity to get a proper education and she had four kids, so surely that was a very hard decision for her to make.

I was just a child by then so the transition from my parent's home to my grandmother's house was not very traumatic for me. My mother was with me and my brothers and sister too so nearly everything was the same.

The same year when I was already living at my grandma's place, exactly the 20th of November 1975 I recall being in the living room playing and the television was on. My mother, grandma and one of my uncles were at home too. Suddenly, my mother started shouting and called my uncle whilst looking at the news on the television. My grandma entered the room worried; all of them started to be very agitated and spoke loudly.

"Oh my God! Finally! Go to hell!" said my uncle Andres.

"That cannot be true, we need to verify this! ... Where are you going Andres? Don't do anything stupid until we know it's true!" shouted my mother while my uncle was running down stairs.

I could not understand what was going on. I was too little to know that the news just revealed was that Francisco Franco the Spanish Dictator died at the age of eighty-two. My family were left wing, especially my uncle Andres, so for them the news was liberating but at the same time dangerous as no one knew what could happen in the country after his death.

My father, to the contrary, was a fascist supporter of the dictator and had pretty conservative political values. I never understood why my mother married a guy with such a closed mind and prehistoric values. Perhaps his film star looks had something to do with it.

Not long after that, Spain became a democratic country and turned aside from the years of tyranny transforming itself step by step into a modern and liberated country.

CHAPTER 5

HATERS, LOVERS AND AGNOSTICS

What is your opinion about male escorts? Did you ever think about it? What do you really know about us and our lifestyle? Do you condemn us? Do you approve of us? Or are you the type that just doesn't care about the subject?

I have catalogued people into four groups in relation to how they feel about prostitution and escorts.

The haters. They have a strong and clear opinion about escorts. They are disgusted by them and believe escorts have no morals or real values. They find it sick to sell sex for money and they think they are the ones to blame for transmitting sexual diseases to others. Often, the hater's beliefs are connected to religious values of some kind. They will never believe or accept that their local priest, rabbi or imam has been with an escort recently.

The lovers. These will be the clients. They know they can access very sexy guys for a price. Clients are able to get from escorts what they cannot get from others. They think they are very convenient and a discreet option, perfect to fulfil their sexual fantasies, companion needs or just to have relief when they want or how they want and with the guy they wish, without too much trouble except a phone call. For some clients escorts are the only option but for others are just an extra.

The agnostics. They don't have a defined opinion about them. They don't know much about them or they don't really care about this subject. Some of them might be curious to know more but never had the guts to search and speak with one of them to learn more. Most of the time, agnostics are influenced by old stereotypes or by what they have heard in the news or in some film they watched a while ago. Other agnostics might even be tempted by the money fact and have some thoughts about doing the job themselves but never had the courage. Their lack of information and taboos make them afraid.

The carers. They are the doctors or nurses from the clinics where escorts have their tests done, or the social workers from charities that try to support them. They are not judgmental and they have a quite clear understanding about what the escort lifestyle is about. I am sure all of them have their personal opinions about the subject and even some of them might not totally approve the kind of lifestyle some escorts follow, however they help without judging.

It won't be the first time that haters or some agnostics crossed my path. I sometimes receive messages online like these ones:

"But you are a prostitute, how do you dare to date anyone?"

"I am sorry; I don't want to get infected with anything weird."

"How many guys do you fuck per day? More than five?"

"Who knows how many disgusting guys you have been fucking with?"

"That is not a job that is something you just do to get money."

"But you are so smart; you could do any job you wanted to do."

"A teacher should never do sex work, they have to teach morals, and a sex worker will never be able to do that."

"No offence, but I don't really want you around my children."

"You were working already today, would you mind to shower before you come home tonight?"

"Can I have a freebee?"

Then you have the lovers and the agnostic, who usually idealise you. Before I opened my first escort profile I used to have about five hundred viewers / clicks on my personal profile per week. When I changed the same profile with the same photos to a commercial one, I started to get two thousand three hundred clicks per week. That has proved to me that people tend to idealise escorts, thinking that they are sexually more powerful, sex gods and more sexy than others.

In spite of what people may think, to become a good escort you need much more than just a good body, bum or big cock. You have to be very open minded, flexible, patient, have a good understanding about people, be smart and adaptable and of course, good at sex.

Communication is essential. One has to listen and to understand the client's fantasies and demands beforehand. Then you make sure everything is ready and prepared to fulfil your client's needs and wishes. You are there for them, not for you.

The escort's sexual life expands rapidly, as we have many weird requests, fetishes and fantasies that clients might never confess or propose to their partners or any other non-professional guys. The fact that they will pay you gives them the courage to be able to express their dark wishes and desires, and finally to fulfil them.

How many condoms does an escort need per month? The answer is lots and lots of them.

An escort without condoms is like a baker without flour, how could a baker make such delicious cream and succulent éclairs without such an essential ingredient?

Let's be honest here. We men love sex. Sexual encounters have become, since the internet revolution, the bible for the gay community. This revolution brought us more freedom but also distorted the way gay people approach and deal with relationships or dating.

Many guys who do not do escort work have even more sex than escorts. For example, I recently met one guy in his thirties for fun. He has a very reputable job Monday to Friday. We met on a Saturday evening and after having some fun and chilling together he confessed me that that morning he went online and hooked up with one sexy guy, in the afternoon a very sexy couple contacted him and he met them for some wild sex, and after in the evening he was me.

Who can blame him, poor thing? Life is short and he has to suffer abstinence Monday to Friday so hey, have as much fun as you can at weekends! Escorts are no different to anyone else. We have sex with clients but also we have sex in our private lives. The difference is that when we are with clients we are exclusively satisfying their needs and fantasies. Everything is about them but in our private sexual lives we search for what we like or want in sex. But does that make us more risky than other guys with a rich sexual life?

What about the guys who go to a gay sauna on Monday, to a gay sex club in Vauxhall on Thursday, meeting some guys online on Saturday and on Sundays they pray at church with their wife or husband?

When you do this job you learn to demystify things related to sex and sexuality, and learn that everything is relative depending on each individual life style. For example, a top manager may well ask for hard canning and being dominated.

Sexual risks and bigoted sexual values are all blown away when you realised how gay and bisexual people live in big cities like London.

"So do you have another client after me later this evening?" one client asked.

"No I haven't got any other client tonight."

"Ohhh, you told me that you were busy after 5pm today so I thought that probably you had lined up other client later today."

"Well escorts do also have a private life and meet friends, people and socialise like everyone else."

There you go; escorts have to live with that stereotype forever. Most people think that we are just sex machines, twenty four hours a day waiting at home for clients and that our life goes around of just sex, sex, sex, and also that we are more risky than others.

Speaking about risk, for me it is very important to guarantee safety to my clients, to all of them but especially to the partnered ones. If my clients know that they are safe with me they will feel comfortable and they will come back. But it is also a matter of values. I don't want to pass a disease to anyone so I have my tests done every three months to make sure that everything is in order.

Regular visits to the GUM clinic are part of my everyday life as escort, but to be honest if I would not be an escort I would visit the clinic as frequently as I do now. Escort or non escort, I want to know how my health is and avoid any problem that can be treated easily.

Fortunately for me the government also consider escorts high risk so we get priority when being tested, including an exclusive clinic for us called the Working Men's Project, where everything is confidential and free for escorts and we get an excellent service by friendly doctors and nurses that do not judge our job or lifestyle.

They are lovely people, very friendly but also a bit robotic in the way they approach their patients. I guess that comes from repeating the same questions so many times per day, and the fact that they have targets and hospital criteria that they have to follow.

What type of sex did you have with your last client?

What was his nationality?

And the previous one to that?

How many clients did you have during the last two weeks?

How many clients during the last three months in total?

Did you do any dipping or other unsafe activity?

Were any of your clients HIV positive?

How many casual or regular partners did you have sex with during the last three months?

With time I realised that each question follows a certain criteria; for example they ask the nationality of the clients because there are certain countries with more sexual contact risk like middle Africa, and the answers will influence the type of test they do. Each test costs money, therefore depending on the type of answers you give they might do all the tests or only some of them depending on the risk. I always add an African client in my answers or a client who told me that he was positive or some other activity semi risky in spite of not always being true. That way the nurse does not feel guilty for carrying out the full tests and I get a proper check out.

The funny part comes when they have to check your private parts. How many willies and bums of escorts have they seen this week? Fortunately for them their patients are mostly attractive young guys and well endowed, so I am sure the views are quite pleasurable for them, much better than the nurses in the normal clinic downstairs where they have to deal with not such gratifying human landscapes.

The clinic also provides free condoms. Each time I visit them I get hundreds of them, luckily they have king size which are more comfortable to wear, and while they are checking the test results I fill my bag with a lot of them.

When I walk in the street on my way back home with my bag full of condoms I always feel a bit funny. I look at the people in front of me in the tube and I imagine myself telling them that I have two hundred condoms in my bag. I can imagine seeing their faces and reactions. I smile while having such thoughts, knowing how judgmental people can be.

Having that clinic with such good service makes me more confident in doing my job.

CHAPTER 6

FIRST FLOOR, ROOM SIXTEEN

Very often escorts have to travel around town to visit clients in their houses or hotels. We call that 'out-calls'.

Rule number 2: Never travel without confirming the details you got from the client.

Get the hotel name, full address and room number from the client.

Google the hotel to confirm it is the right one and the address is right.

Ask the client where the lift is, so that when you enter the hotel you have a smooth entrance without being noticed too much.

Wear smart clothes, especially if the hotel is a five star hotel. The client will appreciate that.

If the client is new or you are suspicious by the way he spoke, call the hotel and ask them to ring his room so you know he really is there and it is not a fake.

I had a situation during my first year, when a client called me for a hotel out-call. He was in a hurry, passed me the details but I did not have time to confirm the information. I got into the taxi and went there. I was wearing smart clothes and I had all my escort tools including some sex toys inside my suitcase. The taxi arrived outside the hotel and one porter opened the door for me. Suddenly I saw a security guy next to the second door and one security arc like the ones in the airport with a scanner belt. He asked me to leave my suitcase and coat in the belt and pass through the arc. Some hotels added that type of security measure after the bomb attacks in London. I was shocked! He will obviously see the items inside my suitcase through the X-ray.

"All fine thanks!" the security guy said whilst giving me the look of "I know what you are coming here for".

I took my blushing and embarrassment with me and went to the lifts. I pushed the button for the first floor and I checked my clothes whilst I looked at myself in the lift mirror.

I walked through the long corridor and arrived at room sixteen. I knocked on the door and when it door opened an old lady appeared in front of me. Ohhh dear! What the hell is going on here? I had to react quickly

"Sorry Madam, I think I have the wrong floor and room" I said, "My apologies."

I took my embarrassment again and went towards the lift. I was very angry. I called my client. "Hi, I am in the hotel outside room sixteen but you are not there. Actually a lady opened the door and it was a bit embarrassing. Where are you exactly?"

"I am in my room right now. What hotel are you in?"

"I am in the hotel you told me. The Millennium Hotel in Kensington."

"No, I am at the Millennium Gloucester Hotel just next door. Just go outside and take a taxi. It will take you five minutes to come here."

"Ok, see you shortly."

At that moment I could not decide if the misunderstanding was my fault or his, but the truth is that a good escort should always check the details and directions twice before travelling. My client did not pass me the postcode and I did not ask for it. When I checked the hotel online I wrote down the one that seemed to be the right one based on the information I got. This time was the first and last time that I made such mistake. What a coincidence that two hotels with nearly the same name where next to one another. Well life is full of weird coincidences and I learnt that I have to be prepared for them at any time.

Many escorts love to do out-calls to hotels. The possibility to visit great five star hotels, get some drinks or even a luxury breakfast in the morning is an incentive for them. Also there are some escorts who cannot do in-calls at their places so for them it is more convenient to do out-calls.

I asked another escort if he prefers in-calls or hotel visits and he said:

"I prefer out-calls to hotels as in-calls put you at risk of neighbours seeing too many people coming to your home. The client knows where you live and can harass you which is something I have experienced whilst my boyfriend's family were visiting. More importantly is that you have used your personal space to someone that maybe you are not so close to even if they are a regular client. You also have to do the preparation cleaning before and after. The advantage of hotel visits is you get to see many different places, you have the option of being able to leave as you wish with no personal information exposed except your profile and mobile".

I personally don't mind doing out-calls to private houses but hotel visits are not my cup of tea. Each time I go to a hotel I get great anxiety. It is like a knot in the stomach. It starts from the moment I accept the booking and I know where I have to go and it continues until the client opens the hotel room door.

Most clients wanting a hotel visit call at the last minute so you have to hurry to get there as soon as possible.

The preparations for hotel visits are therefore a bit of a roller-coaster for me. I have to do all the preparations and check details in a short time. Get smartly dressed, check address and directions, prepare all the escort tools and call the taxi while preparing everything so the waiting time is shorter. Check the route on your mobile GPS to make sure driver does not get it wrong and text the client when nearby.

My heart always starts to pump faster when I am just arriving at the hotel and I know I have to do my entrance. I hate that moment. I know where the lift is so I always do the same thing. I take my mobile and start 'checking' text messages, faking that I am using it so I can avoid looking at anyone and pretend to be a business man with my smart clothes, my suitcase and my mobile. Whilst I pass through reception and walk towards the lift I can normally hear my heart pumping faster. I enter the lift, push the right floor button and the doors close. Then I start breathing again.

I check myself in the mirror and think about my client now. I get mentally ready for my purpose, to satisfy my client and to have a good time with him. He opens the door and I smile. All is fine from that moment. When I finish and leave the room I have the opposite feeling to my arrival. I feel free, relaxed and happy. I have the money in my pocket, my client is happy and the mission was achieved.

I never understood the reason behind my stress entering hotels to meet clients, but after a while I learnt to do it mechanically. I now have a discreet and smooth entrance without being noticed too much, but the anxiety is always there.

Out-calls to private houses are very different for me. I know the client will open his door straight away and other people won't be around or involved. On the other hand for me hotels are very impersonal and boring, everything looks the same and I always have to be careful about not creating much mess when playing kinky.

In a house you can relax and play as you want. Houses are more personal and most importantly you can get more details and information about your clients by observing their houses.

Rule number 3: A good escort always observes and listens.

The more you know about your client the more understanding you will have about what he is like and get small crucial details. That information might help you to understand him better and will facilitate the conversation and even the sex. It is incredible how much information you can get by observing a person's house and his reactions.

CHAPTER 7

THE VISITS 1977

My mother went to find a job soon after the separation. She knew that in spite of the help from my grandmother and the small money allowance my father was obligated to provide for us, she would need to work to support four kids.

She had a limited education and no qualifications so decided to go from shop to shop for many weeks asking for a full time job. After many rejections she found a shop specialising in luxury fabrics, making all sort of items like curtains, beddings, cushions, upholstery, etc. They wanted a reliable seamstress for their workshop and the fact that the owner was a very strict catholic lady helped my mother to get the job.

The first years of separation were very turbulent and I remember my father coming to my grandmother's house many times, shouting and insulting my mother from the main stairs or banging on the door. He could not accept that his wife had abandoned him and he was convinced that it was all temporary and she would come back to him, 'the man'.

My two brothers and I were obligated to see him twice a week as we were under age, but my sister, who was over eighteen, decided not to see him anymore.

My father used to pick us up with his car and take us to a park or to the cinema, but before that we had to spend three or four hours sitting inside the car being interrogated one by one.

"So how many men did your mother meet this week?" my father asked my older brother Juan who was in the front seat with him

"No one father" said my brother.

"Do you think I am stupid or what? I know your mother is meeting other men, tell me the truth!"

"I haven't seen her with any man father" said Juan while my brother Antonio Junior and I were looking at the scene from behind knowing our turn would come soon.

"I know what your mother does! She throws a rope down from the balcony at night when you all are sleeping and men climb up to the flat to meet her. What a whore she is! That is what she wanted, to be free to meet other men! Am I not right?"

This scene and kind of questions went on and on for hours during each visit , until one of us, exhausted by the interrogation and my father's aggressive manner, confessed falsely that my mother was seeing other men, just to be able to get out of the car and go somewhere else. This scene was repeated each time we met my father during the first three years of separation.

I remember one time when we arrived back home from one of my father's visits, my mother asked us if everything went ok and my brother Antonio exploded in anger and started crying and shouting.

"I never want to see that beast again!" said Antonio. "One of your sons told him that you are meeting other men and he went nuts. We had to stay answering questions and questions for hours even though what we said was false."

My mother held my brother in her arms while he was crying

and I remember her frustrated and sad look knowing that she was not able to stop my father from coming to collect us as we were under age still.

CHAPTER 8

THE CHRISTMAS TURKEY

When you do this job you have to be prepared for all sorts of requests.

This is what a client texted to me online [sic]:

Client: "*Hey, got a fetish I want to explore? Want to be prepped like a Xmas turkey, pubes plucked covered in lard, squeezed into my levis, stuffing squeezed up my ass and in my mouth, beaten with mallet to tenderise, tied, pissed on, wrapped in cling and left somewhere hot ,then stuffing scooped out and pricked all over and carved, I know extreme, but can u do this?*

Would like you to carve off my levis after you pick me all over, U cud stick a carving fork in me while u do it and would like the stuffing squeezed up from a piping bag nice and hot and a sounding rod up by cock like skewer. How else mite u carve me ....U cud stick in a piss tube and make me hold till I'm done then baste me with what u drain off."

Pedro: "*I will be happy to do it for £400 if you get the materials needed, cling film / stuffing / sounds / carving knife etc or £500 if I have to get the materials.*"

Many guys won't accept such a request but for me the challenge and the satisfaction of making my clients fantasies real are irresistible. Many clients have weird fantasies but soon they freak out and can't do it or cancel last minute. I always make sure that I get money in advance or at least part of it. The client agreed to pay the materials money and some extra in advance, so once he sent £200 via PayPal I organised everything for him.

I used huge plastic sheets from B&Q, the ones used by painters to cover carpets and flooring while doing paint jobs. I covered my bedroom floor and furniture with it.

I wanted to make it as real as possible, so I did some research online about turkey stuffing and recipes to get some ideas. I also printed photos of roasted turkeys and put it in different places around my room to create the mood.

All the utensils were prepared on the top of the bed so the client could see them on arrival.

When I opened the door I saw a chubby man in his forties, quite tall, a bear type of guy wearing jeans and a t-shirt.

"Finally, my turkey has been delivery! I was wondering when it will arrive. I have everything prepared and I want my turkey to be moist and succulent so I will start preparations straight away!"

When the client entered the room and saw all the plastic and utensils he looked at me and nodded his head, smiled, giving me the approval. I smiled too and asked him to remove his shirt and to lie down on the floor on his back.

I asked him to open his mouth and I pushed one small apple inside. I asked him to bite it and keep it there.

I arranged in advance some videos on my computer with Christmas music and also Nigella, the sexy chef, making turkey recipes for Christmas time. I started playing them to get in the mood nicely.

"But what is this? How is it possible that my turkey is full of hair everywhere? I thought I bought the finest turkey! I cannot cook a turkey with hairs on it! What are my guests going to think if they find a thick hair on their meal? We need to sort out this immediately."

I took some depilation strips from thc utensils and smiled while waving them in front of my turkey face. "Oh yes! Let's make my turkey soft, smooth and hairless."

I put the strips on his chest and tummy and ripped them off at once. The turkey was scowling in agony and biting his apple but I could see in his eyes a blink of satisfaction.

"Ohhh look at this lovely turkey, much better now. I think we are ready for step two. After removing every hair we need to moisten that skin so it gets crunchy and shiny during the roasting."

I went to the kitchen and warmed up a bowl of lard in my microwave. Once it was dissolved and in liquid form I took a cooking broche and started to spread it all around my turkey's skin, including the face. The situation was perfect, as at that precise moment Nigella was describing in her video how important is to lard the skin of your turkey to get the best results.

"Well, now comes my favourite part, the stuffing! I want my guests to be happy so I bought the best one I could find. The finest stuffing with apples, walnuts, onions, currants and parsley. Ummmm, delicious!" I cooed.

I took the stuffing from the bowl and inserted it inside his mouth after removing the apple. Then I put the apple back in his mouth. "I think my turkey needs more stuffing. I want my guests to be delighted by the flavours."

I opened his trousers and inserted the rest of the stuffing under his briefs and then I closed them up again.

"Well this is looking pretty good. I think it is time to add the last pinches of flavour to make sure my turkey smells and tastes delicious."

I took some fresh sage and rosemary and put it partially inside his ears, inside his pants, in between his toes and in his mouth, in the space left between the apple and his lips. Then I took a spray bottle filled with fresh lemon juice which I prepared before and started spraying the lemon all over my turkey to make the skin moist.

"That's it! My turkey is now ready for wrapping before putting in the oven. What a lovely smell! I am getting hungry already!"

I took the kitchen foil and started to wrap him in it, leaving just part of the face uncovered. He looked lovely all covered up in foil with the sage and rosemary coming out from it.

"Well now we are coming to my favourite time" I said. "I will have a nice glass of port and read the Guardian paper while my lovely turkey is being cooked."

I turned on a couple of desk lamps that I had prepared next to his body and pointed them at him, simulating the heat and light of an oven.

I lay on my bed next to him and started to read my newspaper, sipping a glass of port.

I went to check on my turkey ten minutes later. "Mmmmmm, how nice my turkey smells! I think it is time to remove the foil and let my turkey get crispy and brown."

I removed the foil and kept the lamps on for a while. I continued reading my newspaper and after a while I went back to check my turkey.

"Ohhh, what a masterpiece! My guests are going to love this. I think it is time to carve and prepare the meat slices before they arrive."

I took the big kitchen scissors and started to cut his trousers while prodding him with a big carving fork. I was having a lot of fun testing him with the fork, poking a bit harder each time until he started to complain.

"How lovely! The meat is just as I was expecting, brown and

crispy on the outside but tender and moist on the inside. We need the final touch."

I took a bowl with roasted potatoes and vegetables already cooked and threw it all over him. "I think we're ready for dinner. Mmmmm, this is going to be a pure feast."

The session finished there. The client went to shower and I started to do the cleaning up. He told me that he was impressed and that he had a great time.

Nothing is better than a satisfied client.

CHAPTER 9

A PENNY SHORT OF A BOB

Meeting young clients is always exciting but most of the time there is something missing, like a penny short of a bob.

I am the type of escort that Middle Eastern men will go for. Many of them, including young Arab boys, often call me for some fun while they spend daddy's money.

The shy inexperienced ones are always very nervous.

I remember one day that I was called to meet a young Arab guy for an out call to his hotel. He did not want to give me the room number and requested meeting outside the hotel instead.

I texted him when I arrived and he called me back.

"Where are you now?" the client asked.

"I am just outside the hotel main door."

"I am outside too, come to me."

"I can't see you and I don't know what you look like. I am just on the left hand side of the main door. Come to meet me here."

"No, I don't want to meet there; if you walk past the door you will see me. I don't want anyone to see us together."

I was starting to get a bit annoyed but I decided to be patient, knowing that this type of client can be very peculiar at times.

"I can walk to the right or to the left. What direction do you want me to take? The hotel is behind me and I am on the left."

"Walk to the right" he ordered.

I walked to the right, passed the main door and saw some people speaking by the hotel entrance, all of them with an Arab look. After forty metres I noticed one young guy hiding behind a lamp post. I started to think that I was in a James Bond movie. I called my client's mobile to see if that guy was him. When he answered his phone I approached him. He was quite handsome, in his early twenties, tall, dark featured, medium built body and masculine but his expression told me he was very nervous.

"Hi, I am Pedro."

"Sorry but I have to be very discreet. I am going to give you a copy of the room key and I will go inside the hotel. After three minutes you will enter the hotel, take the lift and go to room 215. I will be there waiting."

He handed me the key and left. Three minutes later I entered the hotel and went to his room.

"Is this your first time with a man?" I asked.

"Yes, it is my first time. Not sure what to do."

"Why don't we start with a naked massage and we will go from there?"

I had no time to start taking off my clothes when he approached me and started to kiss me. How delightful to kiss an inexperienced boy whose flesh is shaking and wanting to sin.

All Arabs boys I have met are very clean and smell nicely of perfume. I know they also like people that are clean and smell well, so I was wearing my favourite perfume, Armani Diamonds.

Our bodies were soon twisting on the bed and I noticed that he was not sure what to do, so I took the leading role making sure he enjoyed it. I asked him if he wanted to be fucked and he told me that he wanted everything, to fuck and being fucked. The sex was a bit mechanical but I was not expecting much from a beginner. His beautiful face and trembling soft skin was more than satisfactory. We entered into a conversation when the sex part finished, about sexuality and the role of men in Arabic countries. He told me that he knew he was gay but he would never be able to fulfil that side of him if he stayed in his country. He would have to marry a woman and have kids.

When other young clients come to my place for an in-call they are always worried about people seeing them arriving or me having a hidden camera in the room. I have to make great efforts to relax them and make them comfortable, assuring them that I am reliable and I know how important discretion is for them.

But not all of them are shy, I remember a couple of young Saudi clients in their twenties that I met a while ago. They are the worst to deal with. Saudis are confident and arrogant, they try to negotiate your rates and test your confidence.

I found myself one time in a luxury hotel room with a huge bed having sex with this young Saudi. He asked me to suck him off to start with as he was lying on the bed answering text messages on two mobiles phones at the same time. I felt a bit insulted and told him "Hey boy, you can choose your mobiles or me sucking you. You can't have both."

He looked at me surprised and stopped using his mobiles. But two minutes later he started again.

He fucked me while using one of his phones and as he came fast he asked me to do a foot massage for him, while he continued answering texts on his mobiles. I did not want to make a fuss so I did my job and when I finished I decided to chat for a bit.

He asked me questions about London and the gay scene. He confessed to me that he had already been in that hotel for three weeks and was pretty bored. He did not know anyone in London so he spent the whole three weeks walking around town during the day time.

I asked him if he came with some friends or family. He said that he was on his own taking a break from school and that he didn't need anyone. "I can manage with my two mobile phones."

In this kind of situation it is very easy to be judgemental, but that's life. Some people are born in very fortunate families and they are totally spoiled.

The other Saudi was living in a luxury apartment block in the town centre and had a private driver with a big car. He was studying in London on a one year course. He was the type of boy that won't accept no for an answer and was very spoiled too.

He was in his twenties, greatly overweight for his age and very demanding. One day I told him that I won't tolerate him treating me like one of his servants and that he was in Europe now. "Here we treat people in a more civilised manner". Since then he has tried to be more careful, and understands that he cannot play about with me.

Other types of young clients are the straight boys. Sometimes I get calls from youngsters, aged from nineteen to twenty-five, who are straight and have girlfriends but are in need of some sexual release. Other guys are curious and want to try to see if gay sex is their thing or not. They normally ask for just some body contact and oral sex, they don't kiss or go further than that. They will never go to the gay scene or put themselves at risk of being discovered so an escort is the perfect option for them. They choose the type of guy they like and can meet in a discreet way, asking for exactly what they want without complications.

A more interesting experience was with a twenty-four year old from Korea. As with most Asians he did not look his age and anyone would think that he was only nineteen years old.

He looked like an innocent twink with a slender body, totally smooth and soft skin. He was the type of boyish looking guy that many guys would love to give a rough fuck and abuse him in bed, but that was his problem. He is a top and he had the smallest penis I have ever seen. He wanted to fuck me but I noticed that he enjoyed me teasing him and trying to fuck him. However in the end he fucked me and came in less than two minutes. It was barely impossible to avoid the temptation of fucking him. His soft tender skin, his little bubble ass and his delicate teen body were shouting 'fuck me like a bitch!' I remember getting a hard-on that was even painful just by thinking of fucking him hard.

He confessed to me that he found it very difficult to find bottom guys to fuck and that most guys just wanted to fuck-rape him in bed. He was truly frustrated and seemed to be living in the wrong body.

To be with me was like a therapy session for him. I was like the rest, tempted by his delicate physical appearance wanting to fuck him and abuse him. He let me play the role and try but he knew that he was paying, therefore, he would in the last minute refuse and fuck me instead. I could see a smile on his face after he ejaculated and the look of victory and revenge in his eyes. I was for him all those guys that fucked him without thinking of his needs or what he really wanted, but this time he was the winner.

Most gay people follow physical stereotypes. Top guys should look masculine or hairy, rough or robust, and bottom guys preferably smooth and boyish. It does not always work that way though. He found it difficult to accept that not many gay guys would fancy being fucked by a guy with a delicate twink look and a very small cock.

He was born to be fucked but he wanted to fuck. Life is full of contradictions.

CHAPTER 10

THE AWAKENING 1982

My first sexual experience was around the early age of ten, when I discovered some porn magazines hiding in my brother's closet. I remember getting shocked but excited when I opened the magazines and saw all those hunky naked men and voluptuous women willing to pleasure the males' lascivious needs.

The photos were beautifully taken and simulating different sex scenes outdoors or in luxury settings. All males had Adonis masculine figures with huge penises. I got especially interested in the women's expressions that showed clear satisfaction and pleasure while playing with the males erect tools or while being penetrated by two or more guys at the same time. Photo by photo I could imagine how the sexual act developed and discovered different types of sexual positions. What a revelation for a ten year old!

The text underneath the photos tried to get you stimulated more by the sexual scenes, using sentences which most of the time empowered the male position and the submission of the women. I didn't realise that this was a chauvinistic approach in heterosexual pornography but I understand now that this is what many straight men like to watch.

At that point I was not totally aware that what excited me from the photos were not the women's bodies but the men on it. The salacious female faces while pleasuring the men was a big turn on for me. I understand now that I wanted to be one of them and pleasure men like they were doing.

I realised later that I had true innate homosexual tendencies from an early age and the porn magazines worked as a detonator of something that was innate in me. If I was heterosexual I would have been getting turned on by the ladies bodies like my brothers were, but that was not my case.

I had many 'solos' when no one was around the house and I went to my brothers' closet to see what new indulgencies they were hiding from me.

I put them back in the same place and position but I had the suspicion that they knew I was using them too, but never had the courage to confront me on such a taboo subject.

My second encounter with sexuality was at the age of twelve when I met a librarian that was interested in more things than books.

I remember spending many hours at the library reading room as my house was normally quite noisy with all my brothers and sister around. The librarian was at a big table in one corner of the room and in front of him many tables with chairs for people to sit and read or study quietly.

I was a regular and my face was very familiar to him. I recall him being very friendly to me and asking me questions or trying to help me in finding books. One day when the room was half empty he approached me at my reading desk. My elbows were just outside the table and he just had to get a bit closer to have his genital area touching my arm. I was young but the twenty seconds he was touching me, while chatting with me in a friendly way like nothing was happening, was more than enough to make me uncomfortable and realise that something was happening there. I did not move my elbow away.

The next encounter with him happened when one day I stayed until closing time at the library. I was very busy with school work and I stayed longer than normal. The library was about to close and everyone had left the room except me and him. He came to speak to me and sat next to me. After the small talk he came straight to the point, took my hand and put it on his trousers by the genital area. He told me that everything was alright and that I could caress him if I want it.

At that moment one of his colleagues entered the room to say that he was about to close all the doors. I panicked and removed my hand, jumped from the table, took my bag and ran away.

For days after that, I could not stop thinking about the incident. I was not sure about what my feelings were but the truth is that ten days later I went back to the library wanting more.

A new librarian was sitting at the table and when I asked him where the usual librarian was, I was told that he did not work there anymore. I understood then that the colleague saw everything that had happened that day and had reported him. The librarian was a paedophile and I was probably not the only child he tried to play with. But now I know the librarian did not make me gay, I was already homosexual and the fact that I came back for more made me understand that I liked men.

Yes, I am the youngest son of a large family and yes my parents are separated so my father figure was not as strong as in other families. I asked myself many times during my adulthood if I was born gay or if I became gay. After reviewing my childhood and how my sexuality developed I realised I have always had a clear tendency for men from the beginning.

We have all heard stories about adults confessing their early sexual games with friends or family members, including brothers, cousins etc, when they were kids or teens. When boys play with other boys at early age it does not mean that they will become gay afterwards. Actually many heterosexual men experienced encounters with the same sex during their childhood and after got married or live a heterosexual life.

My first early sexual games were with one of my male cousins probably when I was around fourteen and he was ten. We used to play around with our willies when no one was around and experiment with our own ways to get pleasure. It was just foreplay but we knew that adults wouldn't approve so we were very careful to avoid being caught. My cousin is now happily married with a sexy lady but I can see in his eyes each time at family meetings that he remembers everything and he feels a bit embarrassed. It was just innocent early kids games so I don't feel embarrassed at all.

I remember during my teenager years going to obligatory religious classes and the priest asking us to go to confession with him. All students queued to kneel in front of the father and confessed. He told each of us that boys who masturbate will get blind and I remember thinking that I should be at least full body paralysed after all my naughty activities, but I wasn't.

I guess I was a naughty boy from early age, wasn't I?

CHAPTER 11

IN BED WITH HIS HIGHNESS

Diplomats, ambassadors, business men, celebrations, cocktail parties, false smiles, gossips about the biggest diamond ring, references to the Prince and comments about his Spanish friend. Power meets power in a luxury resort with the smell of curry and happy flies on the air.

The first time I met a VIP client was in the French Alps. He spoke to me online and asked me to fly to France on the same day. Everything happened so fast. I normally don't travel abroad at such short notice but my intuition told me that he was a genuine guy. We spoke on the phone and then he booked the flight ticket and arranged for a driver to pick me up at the airport.

I had no clue about who I was meeting or where exactly I would stay. I was just told that I would be staying with him for two nights at his holiday house. He seemed very confident and relaxed on the phone and he clearly knew the steps to follow when booking an escort, so obviously I was not the first one.

A driver on his forties with a masculine Arab look, named Hassan, was waiting for me at the airport. We made small talk about the weather and he asked about my flight, I answered politely but

I was silent for most of the journey while I watched the beautiful Alps through the car window.

I was a bit nervous as I didn't know who I was meeting or where, but what I knew for sure by the way he approached me, is that the person I was meeting was a VIP client and very wealthy.

The driver parked the car in front of a beautiful wooden house typical of that area. The house was situated on top of a mountain with magnificent views of the Alps and the valleys. Two young Indian guys were waiting at the main door and they took my luggage. I was nervous as I was just about to meet my client, but I tried to appear calm.

The driver started to give orders to the Indian servants and asked me to follow him. We passed the hall and entered a large room full of paintings and antiques. I saw a man laying on a design divan chair and wearing a silk embroidered bathrobe.

"Mr Pedro is here, Sir." The driver stated.

The man approached me and shook my hand. "Welcome to the Alps, Pedro. Did you have a good flight?"

"Yes, thanks. Everything was very fast but I am glad to be here."

Mike was tall, robust with dark features, in his late forties, with very refined speech. He had certain peculiar mannerisms and a very strong presence. His face seemed a bit enhanced but I could imagine how handsome he was years before.

After some small talk and drinks on the terrace with views of the mountains, we went to the bedroom where I had a shower. He was waiting me on the bed and I offered a massage which he accepted by just turning around naked on the bed. No words were necessary and evidently I was not the first proposing him a naked massage. After the massage we started kissing and had sensual passionate sex. He especially enjoyed it when I got a bit rough and dominant but I knew that was just part of the game and he was not really into it.

He decided to have a nap after sex and told me I could do as I wished. "Jahim, the servant, is there for anything you might need."

I went to have a cigarette and read a book on the terrace. On my way there I had the chance to have a look around the house. There was a big portrait of my client in the main lounge wearing very elegant Arab clothes, beautiful chandeliers hung from the ceiling, antique furniture mixed with contemporary and all sorts of other beautiful objects; antique jars and candelabras where everywhere, but what caught my attention was an old book on top of a huge glass coffee table. The cover of the book featured two initials in old calligraphy, the same as in my client's portrait. I opened the book and the whole story of his family and ancestors unfolded in front of my eyes. I was with an Arab prince in one of his holiday homes!

That night I was asked to wear a suit. We had dinner on the terrace with two other guests, a French lady in her fifties, very friendly and glamorous, and an English gentleman who apparently was an art dealer. I kept a low profile and spoke only about subjects that did not compromise my client: my country, my point of view about life in London, French wines and food, some travel experiences, etc.

Rule number 4: Try to avoid conversations related to politics, religion or delicate subjects that might compromise you or your client.

I didn't know it at the time, but this was the way my client tested my manners and capability to be in social events.

This was just the first of many meetings that followed during the next 4 years. Paris at the Ritz Hotel enjoying the same room where Lady Di stayed before she died, El Palace Hotel in Barcelona for a small charity dinner or my stay in Dubai for my first big event.

I remember that I was told to bring a couple of suits and other smart clothes for that trip to Dubai but I had no specifications about what type of event we would go to.

I was staying at Mike's private residency which was in my humble opinion a palace. I had a whole floor of the building to myself including an enormous room with ensuite bathroom. The prince was staying on a different floor. The servants made sure my suit and other clothes were ready and properly pressed before the evening event. The phone in my room rang and I was asked to go to the main entrance where a Rolls Royce and driver were waiting for us. Mike was wearing a beautiful cream Jubba with delicate embroidery, a silk scarf hanging from both shoulders and some prominent jewellery on his fingers. He handed the driver a couple of bags with the name of famous boutiques printed on them and got into the car. I followed and sat next to him in the back of the car.

We did not speak much during the trip and I entertained myself watching the skyscrapers through the smoked windows. The car suddenly stopped, my client looked at me and while getting out of the car and said "Enjoy!"

I realised what he meant when I got out of the car.

There were about fifty photographers with their cameras flashing, taking pictures of us at a red carpet to the venue. My client looked at me again, smiled and winked while starting to walk on the red carpet. I just wanted to kill him. He was having so much amusement just watching my shocked face. All this took me by surprise and I had to recompose myself really quickly as everyone was looking at us. The driver holding the bags and I followed him just steps behind, with our poker faces.

When we got inside I saw a huge reception room with about fifty round tables which were very beautifully set for dinner, each table for ten guests. I could not help but breathe deeply knowing what a long night was waiting for me.

We were taken to our table by the event manager, who very politely told Mike how glad they were that he could make it to the event. Everyone at the table stood when we arrived. Apparently he was the most important guest in the fashion show we were attending. I was on his right, with a French lady on my right and eight other guests around the table. Some of them were close friends of my client. The dinner had ten degustation courses including the dessert; I've never ate as much food in my life! I started to learn how Arabs always like to go over the top in everything they do.

I was exhausted trying to keep a smiley face, chatting with the guests from my table and following the protocol. We had to stand up about twenty times and shake hands with each person that came from other tables to say hello to the principal guest, the Prince. Let's not forget the television cameras and photographers that were around our table like vultures trying to get the best shots.

At that point I started to understand the lifestyle of the mega rich and also how these types of events must be so tiring for him when he is the centre of attention. I couldn't help but think of his possible intimate demands once we are back at his house that night. I breathed deeply again and smiled while watching the fashion show.

That night we spent some time in bed together but the excess of wine my client drank saved me from a long lascivious night.

That day will be in my memory for years. It was my first big high class event and I learnt many things that helped me for future meetings with other VIP clients.

Did the people ask me very personal questions? No, they didn't. They know I am the principal guest's friend and they would never do anything that might offend him.

Did some people guess who I was or what I was doing there? Probably some people did, but most of them just thought I was a friend from London. These types of influential people have friends everywhere so I could be just one more.

Rule number 5: Be affable and a good , but never get too close to your client's guests even if you like them or you fancy any of them. That line cannot be crossed.

I met him at other very big events after this one where I mixed with ambassadors, politicians, princesses, and very important business people. That world is on a totally different level to the normal world and I learnt one very important thing. Rules were made for everyone except for the ones at the top!

☧ ☧ ☧

What a revealing coincidence I had in Paris when I had to meet the Prince. We arranged to meet on a Friday, but I decided to travel there the day before to meet a very sexy guy named Antonio from Paris who contacted me on my commercial profile asking for fun (a freebie). He was half Spanish and half French, tall, very masculine and very well endowed so I accepted the invitation to stay at his place for one night before meeting my client.

What a machine in bed! He didn't seem to get tired and wanted to keep going on and on.

After several hours of fun we started to chat:

"So who are you meeting tomorrow?" asked Antonio

"I'm meeting a regular VIP client."

"What is his name?"

"I'm sorry but I have to be discreet" I said.

"Is he an Arab client?"

"Yes... He is."

"From Dubai?"

I was surprised about his questions. "Yes, how do you now that?"

"Is his name Mike?"

I was shocked when I heard him saying my client's name. He knew where he was from and his name. How was that possible? Antonio noticed the surprise on my face.

"I was his favourite before you" he explained, "I met him for about five years and travelled with him to many places but suddenly he stopped calling. "

I realised then that my relation with the prince won't last forever and other favourites would come alone soon after me.

☧ ☧ ☧

Through the years I have met other important clients.

I had the chance to travel to Nairobi and met a client for companion services during a safari in the African Savannah. I was very worried about this trip as it was my first time travelling to meet someone on another continent. However the client understood my concerns and he was very patient answering all my questions directly on the phone and following all the steps to make the booking.

Rule number 6: When you have to travel abroad, follow your intuition. Get as much information as you can about your client, name and address, places where you will stay , type of events you will go to etc and make a contingency plan in case something goes wrong.

For this type of trip there are many things to organise and prepare before travelling.

Chat with the client as much as you can to create a trust relationship that works both ways and stick to your gut feeling. If something seems wrong then don't take the risk. As they say, if it looks too good to be true then it probably is.

Get the flight and accommodation reservations details, with original copies via email.

Ideally get a reservation fee in advance to guarantee the client is genuine, especially for long trips of more than four days.

Get your travel visa ready in advance; don't leave it to the last minute as in some cases it might take several weeks to be done.

Get your vaccinations done at least ten days before travelling.

Get all the clothes ready that you need, keeping in mind the type of places you will visit.

Get a small first aid kit and basic medication in case something happens.

Make sure you have enough money in your bank and you will be able to use your credit card abroad in case of emergencies.

Check optional affordable hotels in case you have any problem or client lets you down once you are there.

Keep the address of your embassy in that country with you at all times.

The client turned out to be a great guy from the UK who was relocating there for work. He was very nice to me and I had a great time, especially during the safari. There is nothing comparable to the adrenalin rush you get when you have real lions, zebras, rhinos, buffalos, giraffes and other exotic animals just metres away in the wild. Forget the zoos!

A further interesting experience was meeting a VIP client in India. It was funny to stay in a five star hotel next to his house. During the day he used to meet me for several hours for fun, lunch and show me the more interesting places in town, then during the night he went back to his house, wife and kids. I was supposed to be a business man there to negotiate a deal with him and his company. The trip lasted five days and for me it was a big cultural contrast. India appears to be organised chaos. Everything works totally different from western countries and their way of thinking and doing things is quite peculiar and dissimilar. My client acted as a great friendly host and he seemed to be a genuine guy so for me it was not difficult to be nice and pleasure him in every way I could. I was not there to judge him, just to do my job. We became friends and I visited him several times in the following years.

I will never forget my experiences travelling abroad to meet VIP clients. All in all it was a wonderful chance to get a better understanding of other cultures, learn about new places and meet very different and interesting people. I was aware that I was there working and not for pleasure. Some of the trips I did were really exciting but others were exhausting. I will say that VIP escorting is a mix of glamour and hard work at the same time. Nothing comes easy.

Finally I can say that all my VIP clients have been pure gents and treated me very well and with respect. However I cannot forget that I am just one more exotic body in their collection and others will come after me.

CHAPTER 12

AGE EIGHTEEN
1990

Before I was eighteen I played around with some girls but I never had full sex with them. The pressure was there, all my friends started meeting girls and many birds also felt attracted to me.

I remember my first kiss with a girl. I fancied an Italian girl who came to my college as an international exchange student. I chatted with her many times and couldn't stop looking at her. It was obvious that I liked her, she knew it and was expecting me to take the initiative to make the first move, but I was very shy.

I knew the first kiss would come at some point and I had never kissed anyone before. I was panicking just thinking about it. One day I spoke with a friend called Mary, who I knew was already playing with boys. I was so embarrassed to admit to her that I had never kissed a girl but I had to play my cards right and ask for advice.

"I would like to ask you something personal but you have to promise me that you won't tell anyone" I said to Mary.

"Of course, tell me what it is?" she replied with a surprised look in her face

"Well, I would like you to teach me something. As you know I like Laura, the Italian girl, but I have never kissed a girl before, so I don't know what to do when the moment comes."

I noticed Mary getting tense and uncomfortable, but she realised how embarrassing it was for me to confess this to her, so she composed herself and tried to help.

"Pablo, kissing is something very easy and natural. You approach the girl when you're both ready, put your lips together and open your mouth, then both tongues will play with each other, sliding gently in and out of each other's mouths. You don't have to worry about it, all will be fine."

She seemed very sure about the explanation but the truth is that her answer did not make me more confident. I was willing to practice with Mary but it was obvious that she wouldn't do that, so I knew I would have to improvise with Laura when the moment came.

One night after a students' meeting in a bar in town, I asked Laura if she wanted to go for a walk. She said yes and we started walking around and chatting. When we were in a narrow street with just one small light illuminating the darkness, she stopped walking.

"Why did you asked me to come for a walk with you?" she asked, getting very close to me.

I was paralysed, I could barely move while looking at her face in front of me. I noticed the heat coming up from my toes to my head, and my body started trembling. She pushed me against a wall and her body touched mine. She started to kiss me and I followed her. It only lasted a minute but I was in another dimension while kissing her. I guess she noticed that I was not an expert and suddenly she stopped and we started to walk again, heading back to where the other students were.

When we arrived back my friend Mary winked at me and I smiled, blushing.

Just before my eighteenth birthday I got invited by two friends to go to Madrid for a three day adventure trip, to go out and do some clubbing there. I knew my friends were gay and they had the suspicion that I was too, but I was still in the closet so they were very gentle with me.

The idea of being in Madrid for my birthday was very exciting, and in spite of my mother not being very happy about it, I managed to convince her and I packed my things ready for the journey.

My friends Angel and Tony arranged for us to stay at his friend's house in the town centre. When we arrived I was introduced to Jesus, a not very attractive guy and quite plump, and to Jorge, a very handsome muscular and tall guy. They were a couple and in their early twenties. I could not understand why such handsome guy was partnered to such an unappealing one.

While getting ready to go clubbing my friends were already drinking and dancing in the lounge, getting in the mood. I was on the couch watching my friends dancing when Jorge passed by wearing just his underwear. I could see his firm and lean muscular body, beautiful face and his dark black short hair. He was very masculine and smiled at me on his way to the bathroom.

"Come on boys! Let's go to party!" Tony suddenly shouted while opening the door to get out of the flat.

While we were at the nightclub I noticed Jorge in a corner observing me while I was dancing. I smiled at him and he started to dance with me for a bit. His boyfriend was not partying with us.

When we were about to leave I saw Jorge chatting with a group of older men at the club.

"Are you coming with us?" shouted my friend Angel to Jorge.

I saw Jorge making a sign letting us know that he will stay there for a while and meet us later.

We went back to the flat to refresh ourselves after a long sweaty night of dancing.

A little while after Jorge arrived at home very happy and excited. “Look what I just bought!” he said excitedly, showing us a bag with two expensive shirts.

How was it possible that Jorge could get two shirts at such an early time in the morning I thought?

I could not keep my eyes away from him. He was so sexy.

“Hey, we are going to an after hour to continue the party, are you guys coming?” Angel asked to both our hosts.

“No thanks, I am a bit tired and my boyfriend is working tonight so we will stay and rest.” Jorge replied.

“I am staying too” I said, “You guys can go and party more but I am exhausted and need some rest.”

“You too Pablo? Come on boys! What a group of dinosaurs you are! Ok then, we are leaving now, see you later!” said Angel while leaving the flat with Tony.

Jorge and I were chatting while sitting at the kitchen table; I told him that it was my birthday and he brought a muffin with a candle on it and asked me to blow it. We both laughed. His boyfriend was in bed sleeping already.

“Well I’m starting to get a bit tired” said Jorge with a yawn, “Perhaps it would be a good idea to go to sleep now?”

I assumed that I would sleep on the sofa in the lounge and Jorge with his boyfriend in the main room.

“Yes I’m feeling tired too” I said

“But there is a small problem... My boyfriend is sleeping already and I don’t want to disturb him as he is working later this evening, so there is only one bed left in the room that we will have to share.”

I was a bit shocked. He was proposing for me to sleep in the same bed as him, right next to the other bed where his partner was already sleeping. I thought he could notice what I was thinking and I tried to calm myself down.

"Don't worry Pablo, my boyfriend does not mind and the bed is big enough for both of us, you can be on one side and me on the other."

I accepted the invitation and we both took our clothes off and went to bed just wearing our underwear. We chatted quietly for a bit and then I moved to one side of the bed to get ready to sleep.

"Pablo, if you move further away from me you might fall off the bed. Get closer and comfy, don't be stupid" said Jorge.

I moved closer to him and I noticed our bodies and legs touching each other. I was excited but paralysed. I could not move. After ten minutes he started to shift with the excuse of changing position and each time his body was getting closer and closer to mine.

His feet started to caress mine slowly and after a while he moved his arm on the top of my back.

This game lasted around forty-five minutes, moment by moment getting closer to each other; touching different part and feeling each other's body heat.

Suddenly he turned around and our faces were next to each other. He leaned forward and started kissing me under the bed sheets. I couldn't believe what was happening, he was so sexy and he wanted me but his boyfriend was in the other bed next to us so I was preoccupied.

"Wait a moment, what about your boyfriend, he might see us."

"Don't worry about it Pablo, he's sleeping. And anyway, he likes watching me playing with other guys!"

I started to kiss him again and moved on top of him. I could feel his cock and it was really hard. I went down on him and started sucking him off. His cock was huge and thick.

After a while he got out of the bed and got a condom and lube. He asked me to lie down and then started to penetrate me after putting some lube in me.

"It's my first time" I said quietly.

He slowed down and started to kiss my neck and my body, while thrusting his hard tool in and out of me.

It was a bit painful but I didn't want to disappoint him so I didn't complain.

When he was getting closer to orgasm he asked me to suck him, and he came inside my mouth while moaning.

I noticed then that his boyfriend had been watching us from the next bed.

When I went back to my city, I couldn't stop thinking about him. I told my friends what had happened and they smiled.

"Listen Pablo, Jorge is an escort and he has sex with people for money. He liked you and chose to have fun with you, but that doesn't mean that he wants anything else. It was just one off for him" explained Tony.

I was stunned to hear all that, but I understood I would never see Jorge again. But he was still the best eighteenth birthday present ever.

CHAPTER 13

WELCOME TO THE HOUSE OF PLEASURES

Meeting clients always involve before and after preparations.

When the clients come for an in-call at my place I practice a routine and make preparations that for me are part of the job.

Shower, moisturise my body and get presentable, unless the client required me not to shower.

Put a clean bed sheet on top of the bed to avoid the bedding getting messy.

Light candles and incense ready to create a cosy atmosphere.

Reduce the lighting and close the curtains.

Prepare the sex toys, sterilise them and put a condom on each.

Condoms, lube and massage oil ready near the bed.

Check that there are clean towels ready in the room and in the bathroom.

Prepare the kinky sex gear if required.

Put music on, depending on the type of session; lounge music for vanilla sessions or dance disco music for kinky sessions.

Put appropriate type of porn on.

Text the client to check if he is on his way or delayed.

Get some water and drinks prepared in case he wants some.

My room and house are like my sanctuary. I spend most of my time here and for me it is not just my living space but my work place too. My room has multiple uses. It is the place where I receive clients, and where I work in my other jobs and projects using my three metre desk and two computers. It is also where I meet my lovers in my personal life. The house is always clean and tidy, and there are nice plants all around the house.

When the bell rings and I open the door everything starts. I smile and welcome the client. I love doing in-calls as I am in my comfort zone and I have full control of the situation.

Also, in-calls are time savers. When going to an out-call for an hour's session, I need to add at least two or three hours extra for preparation time and travel. I make my out-call rate quite expensive to encourage clients to come to my place.

My rates are £160 per hour out-call or £100 an hour for an in-call at my place. I never negotiate or change my rates as this could go against me and confuse my clients. If I charge a client £160 for an out-call one day and he calls me next month and I decide to charge £120 for an out-call because I am not busy, the client would expect to be charged the lower price from then on. Many escorts make this mistake and they lose clients that way.

When the client enters my room everything is ready, including a suitable atmosphere. The candles and incense are on and so is the music, the porn, semi dark cosy lighting and a clean bed. My room is quite spacious, clean and organised.

For vanilla sensual sessions I normally start by offering a drink to the client and having a chat before starting. I ask him the key questions to make sure I didn't miss any information about the type of sex or sexual activities he wants to play.

To start I offer him a sensual massage. I ask him to undress and lay on the bed on his front and the session starts. After about ten or fifteen minutes of sensual massage, when I am already turned on, the sex part starts.

You will probably be asking yourself, how can I have sex if the person is not my type or they are too old? For me age, shapes or ethnicities are not issues. I can manage to disconnect from all that negative approach and I think that he is a person wishing satisfaction, physical contact and affection.

I am there to provide that, and it is my mission during that hour.

I concentrate on the positive aspects about him, personally and physically. Then I take control of the situation and try to read his body language and reactions, focusing on the things he likes the most. For me it is a satisfaction to see he is enjoying it.

There is, in front of me, a person who I wouldn't have chosen if I found him in a gay bar or at a party, but he is on my bed now and we made an agreement. He will get my time and body for a short period in exchange for a financial tribute. The fact he is paying for an intimate service does not mean that he owns me. I am free and I am in control. This is just an agreement between adults. It is a job. I am there to make my client happy and I am satisfied when the challenge has been achieved.

After sex I rarely jump off the bed; I stay for a while with the client there. This is the perfect time for chatting. While I continue caressing his body I start the small talk and ask key questions that will give me more information about him. Where is he from? Is he married or with a partner? What work does he do? And so on. It is not my practice to ask direct questions but I manage to get a lot of information in one way or another.

The best way to finish the session is to offer the client a shower. Then he knows that we are done. He might have one or refuse and start to get dressed. Some clients give you the cash before starting and others at the end. I am flexible on that during in-calls.

Are all my clients older or not my type?

No, sometimes I get men who are very handsome or attractive but they are maybe only 10% of my clientele.

I remember once I opened the door and saw a super sexy guy in his late twenties, tall, masculine and very handsome. I was taken aback but had to hide my feelings. When he undressed I had to hold my breath. He had a straight porn actor body, like a rugby player, athletic and with a beautiful ass and cock. He confessed to me that he had a girlfriend and only did this once in a while. I just wanted to jump on him and have passionate sex, but I had to be professional. After all it had to be about him and not about me.

His sexual requests were very basic and despite the fact I was keen to give him anything he might want I followed his instructions and we played his game.

When a requested session is about kinky or rough extreme sex, everything starts in a different way.

Once the client enters the room, we do not have small talk. He is asked to get undressed immediately, to leave the money on the desk and kneel on the floor. I leave the room while he does that and prepares himself. Then when I get back in the room, I am the boss and I take full control of him.

All the gear necessary for the session is ready in the room and visible to the client, which excites him more. BDSM flog and cane, sex toys, restrains tape, piss funnel, lube, condoms and poppers.

Role play is very psychological and some people might have very specific requests so I have to play based on their fantasies and mixed with my own style. I love to see their faces when they become over exited and they are under my full control. That is the sign. At that moment I know I could do with them anything I wished.

CHAPTER 14

WHAT CRAZY THINGS HAVE YOU DONE FOR LOVE?

I met a very cute Egyptian guy named Akins in London at the end of 2011. He was twenty-five, tall, handsome, a very easy going personality and with a beautiful huge cock. He was on holidays visiting friends and after a very passionate encounter at my place we met several times before he went back home.

We had a love crush and we continued chatting online for a while. Arab boys are unique in making you feel special or like their exclusive possession, which is very appealing and different for a European boy like me.

I wanted to know more about him. I realised that the best way would be to meet him in his own environment to discover more things about him. I saved some money and organised a trip to Alexandria where he lives.

The day before I left news broke that people in Cairo where planning to start protests and revolts against the regime.

I called Akins and asked him about the situation in Alexandria. He told me that everything was fine there and that I would be safe. I did not think twice and got ready for my departure. What you will read next is the diary I wrote during my stay in Egypt.

Egypt – January 26th 2012

Today my holiday in Egypt started. I cannot wait to meet my friend Akins in Alexandria.

The flight was quite pleasant and when I arrived in Cairo I used my charm and managed to convince a driver to take me by car to Alexandria (more than two hours drive away) for just 400 EGP (£40), a total bargain for a foreigner.

Thanks to that I avoided the stress of crossing Cairo town centre on the way to the train station and taking a train in a station I am not familiar with.

Finally I arrived in Alexandria and at the hotel. I checked in and explained to the receptionist that my booking was for two people and that my friend would check in the next morning (he did not know it was an Egyptian man).

They took me to the room and what a surprise! Here I am in one of the suites with sea views; I have a huge room with a large lounge and beautiful views of the Mediterranean Sea.

The decoration inside is like the Ritz in Paris but in an Egyptian style; very classy, a bit old fashioned but very spacious.

I finally met my friend this afternoon. I tried to be patient and to adapt to a slower way of life. This is his town and it is a Muslim country so I am aware that everything has to be discreet and I cannot take up all of his time, as his family and friends are here and he won't be able to be with me all the time.

I also realised that despite his very good manners and his good education, he comes from a very humble family. He wants to introduce me to his friends who are all 'straight' and 'virgin', and all they think about are girls and football, so I am really looking forward to sharing with them my total lack of passion for both girls and football!

I think because I am Spanish they want me to play football with them. Well, they might realise by then that the type of balls I play with normally are other kinds of balls.

Alexandria is similar to my city in south Spain but Arab style; more messy, noisy and chaotic. There are no traffic lights in the whole city. My friend Akins told me that the rule to cross the roads is "to jump into the traffic and pray to God that they will see you and stop". But what about if you are Atheist I thought?

The people seem to be quite friendly here in general. The food, drinks and transport prices are reasonable, better than in Morocco.

The sea front is full of families, boys and girls including sexy teens just chilling by the seaside walking area.

I am very tired after all the travelling, so I will have an afternoon nap in my super room and meet my friend later in the evening.

More to come...

January 27th

After my nap I got an SMS text message from Akins saying that there would be protests in Alexandria that evening and tomorrow (Friday) afternoon at 1pm. He advised me to stay in the hotel.

In the hotel! Alone! I would rather join the protesters, which would be way more exciting! Ohhh dear, what a boring evening ahead!

I decided to go for dinner in the hotel restaurant on the top terrace. What a great place full of candles, lounge music and views of the harbour. I was the only customer so I got excellent and fast service. The whole restaurant just for me! The food was very good and super cheap. A two course meal plus freshly squeezed juice served in a posh restaurant for just £6, can you believe it? I had lentils soup and a mixed grill, mmmm nice!

While having dinner a message came through from Akins saying that he would pick me up with his friends to go to the cinema. Oh dear! At least I know that they won't be able to speak about football while watching the movie.

I might film and take pictures of the protest from my balcony tomorrow.

Akins, who is called Jamie or Jimmy by his friends (he uses this second name because he hates the name Akins and anything related to his country), picked me up in a car after dinner and introduced me to his best friend, a very cute guy with similar good manners to Akins. We went to visit several malls (plans changed as we were late to go to cinema) and they explained to me this is what people do here. They walk around malls or stroll by the harbour when the weather permits it.

Yes, we spoke about football and girls but I was clever enough to refocus the conversation on what they thought about their country and the situation here.

They are both in their middle twenties and they're not happy at all about how things are here. They want to leave their country as soon as they finish their engineering degrees. They showed great discomfort in relation to Egyptian people's mentality in general.

Today is my second day here so many things could happen during the next days. For now I find it more interesting to mix with the locals rather than visit castles and pyramids. On the other hand it won't be very safe to visit monuments right now in the middle of the revolts. Until today the atmosphere here was relaxed but that might change from tomorrow when the revolts will start in Alexandria.

When I arrived back at the hotel I noticed the internet was not working. This was part of the government strategy to stop the protesters communicating with each other.

For now, I am treated like a king at the hotel. Firstly this is because it is half empty and secondly because they are worried about what foreigners might think about the revolts and how this will affect the hotel business if we give bad reviews.

When I speak with the workers in the hotel they try to minimise the worry but as soon as shouting starts in the streets they all jump to watch or even join in.

Today I realised Akins plays the role of leader with his friends.

They respect him and they listen to what he has to say. I can see clearly he has a strong intention to move abroad as soon as he finishes his studies. I wonder if for him I am that possible door to enter Europe or if he has genuine feelings for me.

I have to recognise that his patience and charm have touched me but I want to see more and spend time with him and his friends.

More to come later.

January 28th

Today is the day of protests in Alexandria. I woke up early and had breakfast in the restaurant, which not many customers were in.

After breakfast I decided to walk in the town before the protest to get used to the area and do some shopping. On returning to the hotel when the praying service at the mosques finished at about 1 pm, the protest started and many people were gathering and shouting down by the harbour. The police were launching tear gas. The hotel manager said that everyone must stay inside the hotel for safety. Internet and mobile phones signals were cut.

From my balcony I had a great view of the beginning of the protest. The number of people protesting was no bigger than five hundred.

I would rather use all that testosterone and adrenaline in the veins of Muslim men in another way.

Akins asked me last night to stay in the hotel during the protest and I jokingly said that I would join the protest.

"Don't call me if you get injured" he said.

What a gentleman!

Here I am, trapped in my hotel alone, watching the protest from my balcony and the Muslim TV news.

I can't really blame Akins for not being here though, because his family wouldn't allow him to be away from home during the protest. At least that is what he said. Maybe he is protesting!

It is 5pm now and I am still in the hotel. I thought the protest had dispersed but right now several groups of about a hundred each passed by the hotel shouting "out Mubarak" and breaking glass on their way down to the harbour with wooden sticks.

I can see the older men asking the youngest to control the violence but in a situation like this no one wants to listen. A group of them are carrying a body using a piece of cloth with two wooden sticks on the side. I used the camera zoom to see the body closer. He is dead. I am taking a lot of photos and video clips while they pass by. The dead man is being used as a martyr by the crowd and this creates more violent responses.

All the small groups are gathering a half mile away at the harbour so it looks like more is to come tonight.

This afternoon I met a couple in their sixties from London. They saw the good reviews about the top terrace cafe in my hotel and came from another hotel to have some coffee here. Six hours later they were still imprisoned there as nobody was allowed to leave the hotel. The man had diabetes and all his medication was in their hotel.

I started to get worried that he could have a diabetic fit after many hours without medication. They were a lovely English couple, but I noticed they didn't have the strength to confront the hotel staff or to request being moved to their hotel. They were shocked by the situation. They had been told that they would have to stay until the next day for their safety but nobody offered them a room or any kind of comfort.

I went to reception and asked to speak to the manager. He already knew me as we spoke today when he came to my room to explain about the situation and the safety measures.

I had to be tough, firm but polite and calm while speaking with him. He appeared to be very stressed so I explained to him slowly the situation about the couple. I made him directly responsible if the man suffered a diabetic fit and fell into a coma. I proposed that he provided a taxi to move the couple in a discreet way so no other guests could see them leaving. The result of not doing that would be to have a guest from another hotel that might become ill, possibly due to his negligence. The pharmacies were all closed and to call a doctor in the case of an emergency would be very difficult with the revolts going on.

I could see in his eyes that he did not want to take such responsibility and immediately started to shout at the staff to provide a taxi.

The couple were finally able to leave the hotel in a James Bond movie style. They were very grateful and happy to finally leave after so many hours.

I'm totally fine and safe in the hotel for now, although the internet and phones are cut so I can't connect with anyone or speak with my family to let them know I am fine.

I will have a relaxing bath and go for dinner on the top terrace later.

More to come.

January 29th

I can now feel that I am in the middle of a revolution.

This morning I was allowed to leave the hotel. I went to town to buy some stuff I needed. Waking in the street I passed protestors.

The civilians seemed to be agitated and I noticed that there were no police around, only military presence standing around doing nothing.

Mubarak spoke on TV last night to the population saying he would make changes but the protestors want him to resign.

Groups of civilians with banners around their arms are taking the role of traffic controllers. It now looks like a pure anarchy. Walking around I could see various cars in the middle of the road that were totally burned out. I understand now where the smoke came from last night.

The protest is getting bigger and bigger in the early evening. People leaving work are joining in big numbers.

I spoke to locals in the shops and they told me they won't stop until Mubarak leaves the government.

My friend Akins did not call yesterday during the whole day. It's true the mobiles and internet were cut but land lines were still available and he could call the hotel, but he didn't.

He called me today just to inform me that he won't be able to come to the town centre as there is no transport available, although I saw the taxis and busses running normally this morning.

I don't feel unsafe for now at the hotel, it's well protected and the protestors are not hostile to foreigners here at the moment.

After a long day of protests all around Alexandria, the situation has calmed now during the night.

The police force has disappeared and only military tanks and soldiers are present in the town but they are not getting involved, they're just there.

The protesters have decided to create mini guardian groups to protect neighbourhoods. I just saw three groups of six guys with wooden sticks outside the hotel.

I was told today by the receptionist that some criminals are taking advantage of the unknown political situation and making robberies and raping women both in Cairo and Alexandria. For that reason they decided to have guardian groups as nobody else was keeping order or protecting the civilians.

The police force had motivated violent reactions amongst the crowds during the first days of protests. Once they went away the protests took place more peacefully but the cities were left unprotected. This was a good move from the government to avoid a crescendo of violence. The situation was very uncertain and I was not sure civilians would be prepared to cope very long controlling their own cities.

I am starting to get worried.

January 30th

When I booked my 'love' holiday I made two hotel reservations, one in the town centre and the other outside town in a tourist area. I am moving to the second hotel today. It will be far from the town so I won't be in the middle of protests any more. On one hand that will give me a rest from the revolts but on the other hand I won't know what the real situation is.

The internet is still cut but mobile phones are working with the exception of sms text messages.

Akins is not answering the phone this morning and I have the impression that he won't come as promised when I will check out at 11am to move to the new hotel. I don't think he is putting into consideration that by coming to visit him I am not only spending a lot of money, but I am also putting my life at risk. He's not making me feel special at all and I've hardly saw him so far. I understand the situation is exceptional with the revolts going on but he is not making an effort even to call and chat with me while all this is happening. I topped up his phone so he could not excuse himself by not having credit, but in spite of this I feel a bit ignored.

Regardless of all this I do not regret my visit to Egypt as I'm learning many things. The local people are very nice and I am by the sea with nice weather. I am sure that in another kind of situation I would be able to enjoy it even more, but I am trying to be positive and get the best of my time here.

I went to the new hotel but felt very uncomfortable there; everyone was very agitated and the room was three times smaller than in the previous hotel. I decided to speak with the manager and explained to him that I would prefer to move back to the previous hotel as I was closer to the Spanish Embassy, transport options and updates of the situation.

I checked in again on my first hotel and had a chat with the manger that was becoming very friendly with me after all that had happened.

I couldn't access internet so I called my friend Patrick in the UK who helped by calling the airline company to check if flights were available. All flights were cancelled for the next two days but flights were leaving on Tuesday and Wednesday, when I was supposed to fly home. But no one could guarantee flights as the situation was very unstable. I called my embassy, which were really nice and friendly, and reported to them my name and location.

I think I was one of the last customers in the hotel but at least I have been allocated the royal suite again.

I am fine and feel safe for now while I am here, but am starting to feel bored and lonely.

I called my 'friend' Akins and he finally answered the phone. He told me that he had to guard his house all night to protect his family and that he won't be able to come to the town centre today.

Now I'm not sure if I am being selfish, but I could do with some company right now and it really bothers me that he didn't contact me even to ask if I was safe.

I feel very disappointed now.

Luckily I am a confident and positive person so I can manage this type of situation on my own but I was reaching my limits.

What is happening in Egypt is an exceptional situation. The civilians are fighting against thirty years of repression, and I am in the middle of it.

The lack of police left civilians in an anarchistic situation where streets are unsafe and criminals take advantage of the circumstances. The civilians are now taking turns during day and night to try to control the neighbourhoods, the traffic, the protests and the safety of homes and shops. Groups wearing banners on their arms are taking the role of the police. How long can they sustain this situation? Some of them cannot go to work while others have to stay awake all night to protect their homes and families.

I am amazed how human beings reorganise themselves in extreme situations, giving priority to safety, family and protection of personal territory and properties. More or less what animals do in the wild?

I have been calm until now but tonight while writing this in my hotel room I heard gun shots outside for first time. I saw a military tank and policemen shooting in the air while passing through the civilian guards on the street. It is the first time in my life that I've heard and saw gun shots so close. It's really frightening as you are conscious of not being in an action movie but in real life situation where people can get killed.

My intuition tells me that things are going to get worse during the next few days so I have to make a plan to get out of here carefully and as soon as possible.

January 31st

Today I got ready to leave the hotel after breakfast and go to buy credit for my Egyptian mobile phone, for emergency calls and to visit the Spanish Embassy.

The hotel's duty manager did not want me to go out but when I insisted he offered one person from the staff to escort me.

Azmi, my escort, was very friendly and helped me to buy credit in a shop. Walking in the direction of the Spanish Embassy I could see the gravity of what had happened during the previous days on the streets. Many police cars were totally burned in the middle of the streets, the government building collapsed and destroyed by fire and some shops with their windows broken.

While walking with Azmi he explained to me that he had not slept during the last two days. He worked at the hotel many hours and afterwards he went home to help the neighbours protect their homes and families from thieves. He then went back to work again without any rest. He doesn't have adult sons, only daughters and wife, so he is the only adult male to look after his family.

I asked Azmi to go for a coffee while I stayed inside the embassy. The Spanish Ambassador was extremely friendly and explained to me that the situation could become very dangerous during the next days. We agreed the best option was to leave early in the morning via car to Cairo airport where a member of the Spanish Embassy was helping Spanish citizens to get a flight out of the country.

The embassy staff took my details and I went back to the hotel with Azmi.

Once I was there I got a call from the Ambassador informing me about a change of plan. The road to Cairo was very dangerous at the moment and I could be stopped by criminals who are taking charge of the roads. The embassy was arranging deals with a Turkish flight agency and advised me to take a flight from Alexandria to Turkey, which was a much safer option.

I went to the hotel lobby with all my documents and mobiles phones and set up office on one of the tables, in case I needed the staff to help me with translations or anything else.

My friend Norman from London was very kind and offered help with the flight ticket. Many calls to arrange everything and inform everyone of my situation started.

I am very lucky to have friends who were keeping an eye on me.

I will do some extra filming while I am here. I can see the potential for a mini video piece or something for the news.

My trip to Egypt is coming to an end and my feelings are mixed. Worry, gratitude, excitement, uncertainty, opportunity, stress.

After two hours on the phone I finally got the flight reservation to Istanbul and called my contacts in Turkey to arrange a room to stay for at least one night.

I am fed up now and want to leave Alexandria as soon as possible.

GET ME OUT OF HERE!

February 1st

Today is the evacuation day. Last night at 4am my sleep was disturbed by the sound of gun shots. I went to the balcony to see what was happening; People were screaming in the street and running up and down and some military tanks were approaching the area fast. The gun shots lasted five minutes but I couldn't see where they were coming from or who was shooting.

I decided to close the balcony and stay inside for safety. I went to bed again, my body was crying for rest.

I went to have breakfast before leaving. The restaurant was nearly empty and not much food was available. There have been no supplies during the last three days so the only food available was coffee and croissants.

The taxi driver that I have arranged the previous day was waiting outside. Alexandria has two airports; the City Airport which is very close to my hotel, and Burgel Airport which is an hour away.

When I booked the ticket they told me the airport was Burgel airport but my intuition told me that something was wrong. I asked the driver to stop the car for a moment and I called the contact agent in Alexandria to confirm. She told me that the information was wrong and that the flight would be from City airport. I was very angry with the situation, how can they make such mistake in a situation like this? I asked the driver to change route and go to City airport.

When we arrived, the airport entrance was fenced off by military tanks and police. The driver spoke with them and his face became serious. Military people surrounded the car and started to look at me and asking me to leave the car. I showed my Spanish passport and explained to them that I had a ticket to Istanbul but they could not understand me. I had their machine guns right in front of my face.

The driver took my luggage and asked me to walk with him. We left the car outside and walked inside the airport. Hundreds of people were queuing at the departures main entrance. Policemen were shouting trying to control the crowds. The driver told me he couldn't go further from there and left after I paid him. The situation was chaotic, people pushing each other and the airport staff were overwhelmed by so many people in such a small area.

I finally found a group of people with the same destination and flight so we gathered together in a group. The process to enter departures, check in and boarding took around four hours, all in the middle of confusion, tiredness, heat, no food, no water and no toilets.

When the airplane finally took off, we started to applaud and smile with a feeling of relief.

When I arrived in Istanbul a driver was waiting for me and took me to the hotel, all arranged by my friends in Istanbul. I was exhausted and my brain couldn't function properly. I just wanted a shower and go to bed.

February 4th

I am at the airport now, on my way back to London. I really miss my house, my bed and my friends. I cannot wait to be back.

My decision to visit Akins was absolutely mad but at least I know now where I stand with him. It cost me dearly to go through a country's revolution to discover this, but it was a memorable experience that I will never forget.

CHAPTER 15

RINSING

Rinsing is the art of the use of seduction and flirting with the purpose of obtaining treats and expensive gifts. This is an art women have been using for centuries and the more sophisticated ones are able to rinse men without even having sexual contact.

Like in the film 'Gentlemen Prefer Blondes' with Marilyn Monroe, many women aim for wealthy men who will indulge them with expensive jewellery and gifts.

Technology has made rinsing much more refined today, where ladies can rinse men through the net without even needing to meet them in person.

Are there men rinsing women or other men? Yes there are, but in this case they find it more difficult to avoid the sexual part.

I discovered the concept of rinsing when I entered kinky sites specialised in master & slave or gay fetishes. I opened a profile as 'Dom master top' with the intention of attracting clients on the site and after a while users started to message me asking for my wish list to send me presents.

At the beginning I didn't understand what it was all about, but after checking other doms' profiles I realised that most of them had wish lists set in Amazon with gifts they wanted.

Some doms even posted photos of themselves surrounded with the gifts they had received from subs or slaves, just to show off and motivate others to send more gifts.

I have never been a fan of getting things from people without giving something in exchange. Nevertheless, with time I realised that for some people it is a turn on and it becomes a fetish to send gifts to people they like, admire or desire.

To feel less guilty I decided to persuade people to send me gifts as exchange for unlocking my private videos. I have twenty private sex videos that I filmed during some of my kinky sessions (with the consent of the clients, of course) and with time many people requested the videos and sent me all sort of gifts from my wish list.

I am not a very materialistic person but I am practical so my wish list was mainly presents I needed or I was thinking of buying myself. Things for my house, materials for my office, extra video equipment, delicatessens, nice bottles of wine, travel vouchers or clothes.

In the same way as prostitution, there was and always will be the existence of people wanting to submit and others to control. The sexual roles of dominant and submissive are not new; they always existed and they are part of human nature.

I wrote a blog in that kinky site related to this subject:

What is a tribute?

A tribute is a gift, a payment, declaration or any other acknowledgment of gratitude, respect and admiration.

Why do you wish so much to tribute your master?

You know what you want as a good submissive slave. You know what you like.

For that reason when you find what you are searching for, that alpha male that ticks your boxes, you can't stop venerating him. It is like an obsession, a mental possession that you wish will become physical too.

You want to be noticed, you want to know him, and you want to suffer under his hands and feet.

You know there are many like you wanting him, it is a competition. You really need to prove to your alpha male that you are willing to be his slave. Firstly you do that by tributes and showing him admiration and adoration, secondly you offer your body unconditionally.

He will then take you and test you, pushing your limits, enjoying watching you crossing barriers that you never imagined before, bringing you to new levels of pleasure and submission.

The bond is established then but your work does not finish there. Remember you are just a drop of water and your master is the sea. You will have to prove continuously your admiration and gratitude. If you do not water a plant, the plant will die; so will the bond.

Your alpha male will recognise your devotion and reward you for that in the way you are looking for.

For many of you this type of text might seem ridiculous or you may even question why some people waste their time doing this, but let me tell you, this is the interesting thing about human beings – there is not a rule that defines us all.

In the same way that a man gets pleasure having a blowjob from his wife; a gay submissive person will enjoy licking the feet of an alpha male he admires, or show his devotion by sending gifts.

I learnt with time that many guys with top jobs involving huge responsibility or being in charge enjoy switching roles and being submissive in their sexual lives. It does not always works that way but in many individuals it does.

I get requests from people working in the financial sector as managers or chief executives wanting to be punished or humiliated or to become your cash slaves (sending you money weekly by request while you humiliate them verbally).

Crazy isn't it? Well, welcome to the real world.

CHAPTER 16

WHEN THINGS GO WRONG

I met Michael in my second year of escorting. I already knew the rules of the trade by then but you often find people who are more clever and twisted than you.

He booked me on the phone and asked for an overnight at his place on Sunday night. He did not hide his mobile number and gave me an address so I had no reason to be suspicious.

Michael was in his early forties, ginger-red hair, a bit overweight and had blue eyes. I normally like to be paid on arrival so when I broached the subject in a polite way, he told me that he would give me a cheque, to which I told him cash only. He said that it was impossible to get £500 at that time of night. He showed me his cheque book and explained that it was his company's account and that I could trust him. He wrote the cheque. I had only two options; to leave or to stay and trust him.

He was very friendly, so I decided to stay. We had a chat and then off to bed for fun. The sex was a bit weird. He was quite demanding and I did not enjoy it but of course I hid my discomfort.

Next day, when I left his place I put the cheque into my account. I was told it would clear in about four or five days. I got some friendly messages from him saying how good I was and that he had a great time.

On Wednesday he texted me again. He wanted to meet on Thursday evening for another overnight session. I was unsure what to do as the cheque wouldn't be cleared until Friday. He seemed polite and pleasant so I accepted and we met again.

The same situation happened with a cheque for the same amount. I deposited the second cheque into my account too.

On Monday, I received a letter from my bank saying that the first cheque had bounced. I texted Mike immediately asking him for an explanation.

His reply was something like this: "How stupid you are, do you really think that I would pay a whore like you? By the way I hope you got tested, as I am HIV positive. Hope you got it too!"

I only play safe but he knew how to play the brain game, planting a seed of doubt in my mind. I had my test done and I was fine but he clearly humiliated me in all ways he could.

Three days after there was a second letter from my bank. This time they informed me that the second cheque had been stolen and that the bank manager was considering closing my account and reporting the matter to the police.

Luckily I was well known to my bank and had a good reputation, so it wasn't difficult to provide a story about a customer who was giving me problems. They believed me as I acted quickly, so they didn't close my account but I had to swallow up my embarrassment.

I was extremely angry and very humiliated by the situation. I resolved to warn other escorts about what had just happened to me and spent two whole days sending messages telling them the story.

Unexpectedly, I had numerous replies. Several escorts had had similar problems with the same client. They were furious too. I took the opportunity to convince them to take action against this criminal and go to an organization which offered support and legal advice for sex workers in London.

Five of us arranged to meet and bring all the relevant documents we had. The adviser at the organization called the LGBT police at once after hearing our stories. We then had a second meeting with two friendly officers. They explained to us that they were already aware of Michael and that they had spent a long time trying to catch him but he was slippery and clever. Apparently many other cases had happened before but the police took a special interest as we were a group complaining supported by a serious organization.

Many months passed after that meeting and the police were still not able to catch him. I was leading the group and the one keeping in touch with the police to check any changes or improvements in our case. This guy was even too bright for the police and changed addresses and mobiles very often. We were aggravated knowing that Michael was free and was doing exactly the same to other guys who were not even escorts, promising them money, meeting them and humiliating them.

Nearly one year later, I was surprised when Michel contacted me online again to make a booking. Perhaps he had forgotten about me? I decided to play the game and see what happened. He wanted me to travel to Wales, where he was originally from, to stay with him overnight in a hotel. At the same time I was chatting with him online, I was on the phone with the police officer in charge of our case. He advised me to accept the booking and inform him of all details so he could send some officers to the meeting place in Wales and finally detain him there.

What followed was like an espionage action movie scene!

I had to convince Michael that I was really meeting him, so I had to play the game carefully and plan properly even to the most insignificant detail. I spent about two hours arranging everything and searching all the details online; train routes, prices and every single stop that train made in case he asked me questions, timetables and arrival times. Also I had to ensure the hotel details were right and have the number on hand in case I needed it.

I told Michael of the train I was taking and the arrival time. He sent me many sms texts messages to check me out but he never realised that I was still at home faking everything. I spent about eight hours on the phone that day answering Michael and informing the police of every step. He kept asking where I was and details of the station I had just passed. I had every detail prepared.

I was supposed to arrive in Wales at 10pm that day. At that time I was with friends at home and they knew what I was doing. I told Michael that I had just arrived at the station and I was on my way to the hotel in a taxi. I even checked the weather broadcast and made comments about how cold it was there at the station to make it more believable.

"I am outside the hotel, where are you? Are you inside?"

"No I am a bit delayed. Why don't you check in and let me know your room number" He said.

Bloody hell, I wasn't expecting that, I thought everything would be easier but he was a very clever bastard. He was a bit suspicious so I had to play an even better game.

I called the police and explained the situation quickly. They rang the receptionist and gave him details of everything that was about to happen.

Everything suddenly became very exciting and intense. My friends were next to me while I was on the phone chatting with the police and Michael.

"Hi Michael, I am in room 10, just checked in. When are you coming?"

"I'm not sure if you are really there or not" he said.

"What do you mean? I'm inside the hotel room. Listen, I've been rushing to meet you and travelled many miles, I hope you're going to show up.

"Well I have the suspicion that something is wrong."

"Listen, I am in room 10, next to reception. Do you want me to go outside and pass you on to the receptionist so you can see that I am actually here?

"Yes, please do."

I was very anxious but had to keep calm and convince him. I had an English friend called Sam next to me who was listening to the conversation. He wrote on a piece of paper 'let me fake that I am the receptionist.' I smiled and nodded my head.

"Hi again, good evening. I have a friend on my phone and he would like to check that I am really staying at your hotel. Would you mind chatting with him and confirm that for me please?"

Michael was listening to that conversation but he did not know that I was chatting to my friend and not the real receptionist. I passed the phone to my friend Sam.

"Good evening Sir. I have a Spanish gentleman here who has just checked into the hotel. What shall I do with him?"

"Good evening. I just wanted to confirm that he has already arrived. I will be there in about ten minutes. Thanks" Michael replied.

My friend did a great job and was very convincing. Michael was on his way to the hotel so I warned the police and they were already hiding outside.

When Michael entered the hotel and knocked on room 10 no one opened the door, so he went to reception. At that moment the police entered the hotel and called his name loudly.

Michael pushed them and tried to run away. He managed to get into his car and drove two streets but the police were prepared and they had another two patrols nearby. After a small chase they stopped and arrested him.

I got a call about two in the morning from the police, informing me that they had finally got their man. I was over the moon to hear that after a long and tense day.

Three months later I received a letter from the prosecuting police team saying that Michael was sentenced and found guilty on twenty-seven different charges. He would be in jail for at least two years.

At last I had revenge and he paid for all the damage and humiliation he caused so many people.

Rule number 7: Never accept cheques from your clients. Cash in hand only.

I have been lucky so far and this was the only situation with a client where all hell broke loose, but there are other escorts who have had similar problems in the past. For example, there was a guy who met a client in a hotel and his drink was spiked. After that the only thing he only remembered was waking up naked on a bed. He had been raped by the client and his wallet and clothes had been stolen. He had to go without clothes to the reception and ask for help. Imagine how embarrassing and humiliating the situation was for the poor man.

Rule number 8: When you are offered a drink, make sure you see the client pouring it, so that he has no chance to spike it. Accept closed cans or sealed bottles only and if you aren't sure, do not drink.

To do escorting is not illegal in the UK but many young guys are worried about reporting any abuse to the police because of their legal status or just plain embarrassment. Many cases are not heard or merely filed away if they have no proof.

CHAPTER 17

TAKE ME TO THE DARK SIDE

Since I have done escorting my sexuality has evolved. I used to be a total bottom but since becoming an escort I discovered not only my top side but also a kinky and dark side too.

There is a huge demand for tops that are dominant and into kinky sexual activities. I have the right look for that so I started, step by step, to research and gain experience of this type of sex.

I started to open profiles on sites specialising in kinky and extreme sex and a whole world unfolded in front of me. Domination, fetishes, role play, S&M, control, humiliation, toys, fisting and so on. I started to meet masters and dominant tops and played the sub bottom role to learn new ways of playing and the essence of hard kinky sessions. Every top and master had their own style of playing but overall I learnt the importance of how to mix and pass from one sexual activity to another, creating the right rhythm for each session.

Once you get into the dark side you learn a whole new sexual language that devotees recognises instantly.

TT (tit torture)
CBT (cock and balls torture)

FF (fisting)
CP (corporal punishment, canning, flogging)
LIMITS
SAFE WORD, etc.

I used some of these keywords in my profiles to attract this type of client and started to experiment my Dom kinky side with them. I created a character called "Dominator", who then became the dark side of Pedro the escort.

I also took some extra photos wearing leather and role play costumes. I started to collect kinky photo examples and showed them to my sub clients to let them know what type of sexual activities they could access. Pedro had the Vanilla profiles which attracted clients into soft standard sex but also had the Dominator profiles, attracting clients who are into the dark side.

DOMINANT AGGRESSIVE SPANISH BLOKE
FOR GENEROUS SLAVES ONLY
MY PROFILE INCLUDES 20 HOME MADE VIDEOS OF ME USING MY SLAVES.

You will be able to see them once you make a tribute and I link your profile with mine.

If you ask me to link profiles without a tribute first I will block you.

When you contact me you must be direct and get to the point.

What do you want from me?

When?

Real sessions can be arranged for generous sluts/slaves.

I am tired of spending time with sluts who waste my time for nothing therefore from now on if you want to play, it will cost you.

The more generous you are the more attention you get..............

DOMINATION
FACE FUCKING
CP / BELT – FLOG – CANE – HAND / MEDIUM / HARD OR EXTREME
BEATING NO MARKS
BEATING MARKS
FEET WORSHIP
TT
CBT
HUMILLIATION
RAPE SIMULATION
AGGRESIVE FUCKING
FISTING
TOYS PLAY
PISS PLAY
BODY WORSHIP
MASTER SLAVE ROLE PLAY
PAIN / REWARD GAMES
LOSS OF CONTROL /BLINDFOLD / RESTRAINT
GROUP SCENES IN PRIVATE

What is not on the menu
UNSAFE
SCAT
BLOOD
NEEDLES
BREATH CONTROL
PUBLIC PLAY OR SCENES
MUMMIFICATION

What am I looking for?
Real sessions
Cash slaves / contact me.

Slave cleaners / contact me
Slaves ready to be abused and filmed by me / contact me.
Slaves already owned / do not contact me

THE MORE GENEROUS YOU ARE
THE MORE ATTENTION YOU GET FROM ME

☧ ☧ ☧

From that moment I started to get all sort of requests for special sessions.

The role play clients, requesting scenes where they wanted me to play the role of school teacher and being canned for being bad boys at school. The doctor role plays, where they are the patient being checked just before an operation. The master and slave where they follow my orders, or the builder role play when I go to repair something in their house and I finish force-fucking them.

This type of session is complicated as acting and costumes are required to make it right. I always have conversations before the session to get a clear picture of the contents and details related to the scene required so I can prepare in advance.

The clients asking for a rape scene simulation which involves normally quite violent and aggressive sex. They sometimes ask me to wear specific items like leather gloves or a mask. Some won't admit it but they just want to recreate a moment or situation from their past and which became a sexual obsession or addiction.

The slave cleaners, who get satisfaction by doing household chores for you and being humiliated. This type of session does not necessarily involve full sex or even sex at all. I have to prepare the session in advance and play the role properly.

The kinky sessions including toys play and fisting. In my opinion fisting is one of the best inventions in sex but unfortunately there are many negative myths about it. Many people think that guys who use big toys and take fisting have a lousy ass. This is far from the truth. The anus is a sphincter that contracts and dilates very easily, especially when trained. Minutes after a guy has been fisted his anus contracts and goes back to the same position.

Fisting is a very intimate sexual activity and involves mental control and training. The bottom guy has to relax and trust the top fister. The top has to play slowly and read the body reactions of the fistee. For me the feeling of inserting my whole hand inside someone's body is strongly powerful, having full control of the pleasure he is receiving.

The clients asking for extreme sessions requesting serious punishment such us beating without limits or being permanently marked. For this type of session I request them to sign a consent form where they specify all the details about the session and explain that they asked for it. These sessions are normally much more expensive than the normal ones; anything from £500 to £3000, depending on the complexity of the scene. I remember one client from Amsterdam who asked for a complex session of five hours including all sort of kinky sex, domination, piss, toys, aggressive fucking, feet worship and being marked at the end of the session with a heated metal marker sign, similar to the ones used to mark cows. He ordered the marker from Germany with a special symbol of his choice and we used it for that session. Who knows what was the reason behind him in getting pleasure by being marked that way. I knew it was not his first time as I saw some scars on his body.

The domination and master-slave role play sessions are the ones I enjoy the most. I have great pleasure taking full control of submissive clients, pushing their limits and watching their lascivious faces full of contentment while I abuse them. I wrote this blog in one of the Dominator's profiles:

The ultimate orgasm (in Latin – ultimate iucunditas), when pain and pleasure meet together.

The art of bringing you to a new level where you have never been.

For me Domination is the bond of gratitude and love from the person submitting to the Dom that frequently, and at times imperceptibly, turns into veneration.

In that moment when I see in your eyes that you will do anything to get that pleasure that you are searching for, when I feel that I took away any remains of your dignity, that I can, from that moment, fully own your body.

I then enjoy the process of taking you alternatively from the path of pain to the path of pleasure.

Looking into your eyes when you are suffering and you're thinking that you can't take more pain but your mind tells you that you have to keep going to get to that reward and that pleasure that's so wanted.

The loss of control is the alleyway to the next level. You don't know what will be next. Your other senses start working faster; you can smell my male odours and the sweat on my body. You are asked to lick my body, worshiping me from my head to toes, from my firm legs to my erect tool of desire.

It will be in that moment when I get you to your highest level of pleasure and I can hear you moaning, when you will suddenly be powerfully beaten and the excruciating pain will mix with the utmost pleasure.

At that point you will have visions and the two "ultimate's" (pain and pleasure) will bring you to a new level of satisfaction, where you will move outside of yourself, like the experience of dying with a smile in your face.

They say in mythology that the ultimate orgasm brings you to the maximum level of pleasure, and it is so intense that it can be compared to what happens when people are about to die and they have visions or they leave their bodies.

But you will come back in this case, and you will never forget such an experience.

Did you get excited reading this text? Did it make you laugh or perhaps you thought that is for perverts only?

Well, deal with it. This is what you find in the real world.

The interesting thing I have learnt about sexuality is that it is very diverse and full of options and possibilities. For centuries sexuality had been full of taboos and repressed, but what harm are people doing in enjoying their own sexuality as they wish, if it is with mutual consent and with other adults?

CHAPTER 18

LOVE AND OTHER FAIRY TALES

For gay people, to find a faithful long term partner in big cities like London is as easy as making a hippopotamus fly. And on the top of that, if you're an escort, make it a whale.

Of course there are many guys 'happily' partnered; but one of them is normally one of my clients or lovers once a month. Sorry!

But what is love, and what is it that gays expect today from their ideal potential partners?

EVERYTHING!

We just can't help it. Our criteria for selection and boxes to tick when choosing a partner is as long as the bible! All that started just after the internet came into our lives and the gay community found freedom to connect with others in one click – dating sites.

Everything started to be about today, the present, what we need now. The prospects of building a life with someone is there floating like an ideal dream. However we cannot touch it or feel it, like we do with the bodies of our new lovers and fuck buddies. The dream evaporates quickly and it is replaced by more fuck buddies.

Our busy lives in the big cities make us concentrate on the

basic and urgent need, sex. We meet people for sex. We might sometimes have a great time and meet gorgeous guys but forget to connect with them on other levels. We also have many other inconveniences:

The guy you just had sex with is already partnered.

The guy just finished a relationship and he is in the mood for fun only at the moment.

The guy was horny and just wanted a fuck, nothing else.

The guy is thirty-four but his mature age is twenty-three, not prepared for a relationship.

The guy is very sexy but too young or too old for you. The age gap may create trouble.

The guy is your age or similar, the sex works and he is lovely but the chemistry is just not there.

I guess you have many other options in mind right now.

Am I a love sceptic? The answer is no, but I became a disbeliever of honest gay monogamous relationships.

I found love several times in my life and had serious relationships but after doing this job I learnt the reality about gay relationships and their dynamics, especially in big cities.

My first real relationship and broken heart was at the age of eighteen in Spain. My gay life was secret at that time, as I was not prepared to come out to family or straight friends and I never looked gay or camp so played that as an advantage. The way I met my first partner was special. I injured my ankle playing sports and I had to wear a cast just before Christmas. I was invited for a New Year's party in the gay scene in my city. I wasn't sure whether to go or not. I called my friend to check the details but some other guy answered the phone. His voice was masculine and sensual and by his tone, a young guy in his early twenties.

"Hi, can speak with Juan?" I asked.

"Yes, but he is in the shower, he will finished in a moment."

"Who are you?" I asked.

"I am Jesus, and you?"

"My name is Pablo. I'm thinking of joining the party on the 31st."

"Mmmm I would love that. I think we should meet, yeah?"

"That would be great. If you're as sexy as your voice I think the answer is definitely yes!"

"Well you will have to check that out on the 31st. I will be waiting for you... Pablo."

"See you then."

Our destiny was already sealed in that conversation.

I took a bus on the 31st to go to the party. I was wearing my cast and my mother was not happy about me going out with my leg injured, but she knew how stubborn I was so decided to let me go. I took scissors with me and I cut my cast off on the bus ride and hid the cast under my seat. When I arrived and started to walk, my leg was hurting but that didn't stop me; after five minutes it warmed up with the walking and the pain went away slowly.

I will never forget the moment I saw him for first time. I was on my own in the club having a drink, everyone was very happy and in a festive mood. I was trying to find my friends in the crowd hoping he would be there with them. Suddenly the DJ pushed the smoke machine button and a lot of smoke covered the place. A person appeared in the smoke walking towards me. The figure became clear once he was in front of me. A handsome guy in his early twenties, tall, masculine, medium build body, brown eyes and hair, looked at me and said with a cheeky smile "Hi, I am Jesus."

He appeared from the smoke looking for me and I was all his, already.

Our relationship lasted a year. He introduced me to his friends and family. The sex was great with him, but I discovered why he was that good in bed. He was secretly an escort, apparently everyone knew except me. I was the good, sweet, healthy, handsome boy and he was the naughty, experienced, dark boy. At that time in my life I was innocent and inexperienced so my only wish was to be with him and enjoy him. I think he started to love me too, but his insecurity about me discovering his secret as an escort and about the drugs and party life style was too strong for him, and he finished the relationship before I got hurt or affected by that kind of life. I was deeply heartbroken and I couldn't understand at the time why he did that. I met no one else for at least a year.

My second relationship was shorter, about 9 months. This guy was a bit older than me at twenty-nine. He had a good job and a huge racing motorbike. A most masculine man and great at sex too, just what I liked. I used to love watching him wearing his red and white leather motorbike suit and holding my arms around him while he was driving at fast speeds. This guy was in the closet too, but much more worried than me about people knowing that we were together so all our encounters were private in the beginning. We had sex in the most unusual places; a snooker table, on a tree in the middle of the countryside, inside a phone box, on the beach totally naked at night, in an empty parking lot or in public toilets. I remember we decided to spend a weekend together and rented an isolated country house (cortijo) in the middle of nowhere. All we could see outside the cortijo were miles and miles of olive tree plantations. We entered the house and didn't even wait to unpack. We threw the luggage in a corner, started to kiss and ripped our clothes off. We had sex for about seven hours with small breaks but never left the bed. Yes, this guy was a machine; he was able to have sex many times in a row and he was a great top, a great kisser and very passionate.

Everything was so intense that we even forgot we had to eat. We then decided to go and find a place to have some dinner. When we came back to the cortijo and entered the room, a strong odour overwhelmed our nasal passages. I can never forget that smell. It was an elixir of sex, sweat, semen and pure hormones all together. We forgot to open the windows and all the smell from our passion and fluids were floating and impregnating the entire room. I wanted to trap that smell inside a small glass bottle and keep it forever.

He introduced me one day to some of his friends, but not without warning me that they were straight and they wouldn't understand our relationship. After that, I think he chickened out and realised that he couldn't keep hiding his sexuality if he continued meeting me. His friends were not stupid and asked questions.

We stopped seeing each other gradually, I was a bit fed up hiding at that point and he was too scared.

My third relationship was the longest and most special for me, lasting three years. I was about twenty-five and was in the UK already. I remember perfectly the day I saw him for the first time. I was working as a barman in a restaurant, part of a modern and stylish hotel in Exeter. I had just started my shift and was stocking the bar for a busy evening. On my way to the stock room I walked past the reception area when I saw a very handsome young guy wearing smart clothes and a tie sat on a chair, alone. My heart started to pump faster. On returning to the bar my eyes scanned reception to see if he was still there. The chair was empty.

Later at the bar I saw the manager chatting with the same guy about shifts and details about the menu. She called me over. "Pablo, let me introduce you to Anthony, he will be the new supervisor".

I looked at him, smiled and shook hands. "Welcome to the team."

He confessed to me after we got together that he thought I was very handsome but he also thought I was straight so he had to be cautious. His heart was pumping fast too when we were introduced.

Anthony was tall, medium build, not muscular but not fat, energetic, brown eyes and medium short hair. He had a sweet boyish voice, was polite and smiley, very chatty and a little bit camp. He was born in the UK but he was mixed race from an English mother and a Greek father.

For many weeks we kept a normal working relationship and distance, but he became a very good friend of my flat mate Rosa, a Spanish girl, who was a waitress in the restaurant too. I remember watching him every day from the bar while he was working. Each day there was something that attracted me more and more to him. He was younger than others in the team but as supervisor he had to give orders. I noticed that he had their respect by working harder than them and by using his sense of humour. He got on very well with all the female staff and I think everyone knew at that point that he was gay so they felt comfortable with him.

On many days we used to walk together with Rosa on our way home, as his house was nearby. One day I decided to invite him in for drinks after work with the excuse that Rosa would be there. He said yes and after many drinks together with other friends we finished at our place. There was just Anthony, two girls and me. We noticed that the people next door were having a party and the girls were very drunk at that point and proposed to go there, knock on their door and get into the party. Anthony and I looked at each other smiling. The girls left the house, so I was alone with Anthony. I said I would show him the rest of the house and he nodded his head approvingly. After a fast tour we finished in my room.

"Well Anthony, this is my room, and now we have two options. I can close the door or can keep it open, what do you want me to do?"

Looking into his eyes I noticed he was shocked by my direct question.

"I have a partner, but we are about to finish" he said.

"So?"

"Close the door" he said.

"I am bottom" I told him.

"Good for me."

We had passionate sex that night and afterwards we went to see the girls downstairs. Following that special day he left his boyfriend who was having lot of alcohol problems, so it was not difficult for Anthony to leave.

He confessed to me that he used to see me walking passed his street from his window on my way to work every day. His boyfriend used to get jealous when Anthony pointed me out and said "look at that sexy guy." He didn't know then that his destiny was already written and he would apply for a job at the same place I was working.

In the next year and a half we dated but didn't live together. It was after I got a better job as manager in another company and I was able to afford a better flat that I decided to propose that we lived together. The new place was a luxury flat with enough space for us, a huge garden surrounded by roses, not far from work and next to a beautiful park. I think he wasn't sure about the move but he was having huge troubles with his flatmate and landlady so he decided to accept my offer.

When you live everyday with someone, so much can change. Both of you have to compromise to make things work. I am the type of person that once I get to the point when things are as I like and the system works, I don't need to make changes for a long time. Anthony on the other hand was the opposite, he needed change constantly. I remember coming home from a long day at work and college to find all the furniture in the flat totally rearranged. I was shocked at first but then I realised that the set up was practical too, so I decided not to make a fuss about the change. That happened every two months.

We followed our routines and I concentrated on my studies and work. I wanted to go to University in the UK so as a foreigner I had the double pressure of being fully prepared. I guess after all the troubles with his alcoholic ex-boyfriend, I was like a blast of fresh air for Anthony's family. Pablo was a healthy guy, good cook, very focussed, working full time with a good job as a manager, studying at college, and living in an excellent flat. They were very friendly with me at all times.

Perhaps, being too focussed and organised put pressure on Anthony and he started to compare himself with me, creating insecurities and developing a problem.

One day after dinner, Anthony went straight away to the toilet. A little voice told me to go check him out so I followed him. I put my ear to the bathroom door and heard him vomiting in the toilet.

I decided to chat with him and asked if that was the first time. He answered no. He was bulimic.

After that our relationship became a rollercoaster. He lost job after job, started to lose a lot of weight and got obsessive with calories, food, diets and extreme exercise. He had a great athletic body at that point, but in spite of that I remember him looking at himself in the long mirror in our bedroom wearing just his underwear, pinching his fatless skinny stomach and saying "Can't you see? I am fat."

I didn't know what to do. I was deeply in love with him but the situation was spinning out of control. Dealing with anorexics and bulimics is difficult even for professionals, as people with eating disorders lose total perception of reality and they need full supervision. By then I was paying for everything in the house, rent, bills, food, etc and so immersed in work and studies that I wasn't able to keep an eye on him enough.

The fights and arguments started to get worse, especially when he spent whole days at home on his own watching TV, eating snacks and vomiting automatically afterwards. I had no other option but to call his family for help and ask them to take their son before it got worse.

The move was the right one. He started to recover slightly step by step, as he had more supervision from his family at home and no pressures or responsibilities for a while.

We continued dating but things were not the same anymore. During our three years together Anthony cheated at least twice on me. He confessed when I caught him out once, but I was so in love with him that I accepted the situation. He never understood why I wasn't jealous. I never needed it to cheat during the three years, for me he was enough.

The day to start university came and we tried to continue the relationship at a distance. We both knew however that it wouldn't last long and we decided to finish after a while.

All these relationships happened before I started escorting. But did I have any partners while doing the job? The answer is yes, I met some guys but none lasted excepting one.

I met Tadeu, a Brazilian guy, online. I remember he didn't have pictures on his profile but from his answers my intuition told me I should meet him. When I opened the door I saw a guy in his early twenties, pleasant looking, nearly as tall as me, medium build, brown beautiful shiny eyes, stubble, a great smile, casual clothes and a cap hat. After the usual introductions I could not help but get passionate and start kissing him. I felt a connection instantly, that man was pure passion, a great kisser and he liked to take the lead in bed, just what I liked. His hands were pure dynamite, his mouth fresh water, his body was not muscular but strong, his skin smooth like a baby marked by two small tattoos and a couple of piercings, a beautiful bubble ass and the greatest thick cock.

Our bodies crumbled into infatuation every time we were together. We were like magnets that locked together each time our bodies were close to each other. From the first day we knew that we wanted more, and he made it clear that he was not looking for just a one off.

On my third meeting with him, I decided to play all my cards, asked the key questions and confess my profession. I told him about my job and asked him about his passport and legal situation in the UK. He told me that his sister in law was a dance stripper and he didn't mind me doing escorting if I was safe. He also told me he had a working visa for two years and he was applying for an Italian passport as he had family there, so that way he could stay in Europe.

My worries went away and we started dating seriously. We used to meet twice a week and I introduced him to my friends and afterwards he introduced me to his family, his brother, sister in law and cousin, all Brazilians. All my friends adored him. Tadeu didn't have a model look like other Brazilians in London but he had a great personality and charisma. He looked like any young guy that you could find at the Glastonbury festival. He was smiling all the time, and knew how to connect with people very well.

I started to fall deeply in love with him after several months together. I remember one night after passionate sex at my place, when he was sleeping; I woke up and started looking at him. His face, torso and legs were exposed. I took my camera and filmed him sleeping. He looked like an angel, relaxed, with that beautiful smooth skin and his firm body resting and breathing slowly.

I used to meet my clients the days I wasn't with him so we never entered any serious conversation about my work, but I had a request from one of my VIP clients to travel abroad for five days to Dubai for a special event and I had to tell Tadeu about it.

He seemed ok with it but when I came back from that trip his attitude was different. I tried to meet him but he was avoiding me. His approach wasn't the same and I knew something was wrong. He finally confessed in a text message that he was suffering and he just couldn't cope with me doing my job. I was upset he was telling me this after ten months together and when I was already deeply in love with him.

Part of me felt hurt and offended, but I really loved him so the fact that he was suffering made me very sad, and I let him go. One week later I got a message asking me to meet in public to chat. My heart was pumping with the hope of him wanting to get back together. We met outside Green Park Station and he suggested a walk through the park. We sat on a bench and he started to talk.

"I love you but I am suffering a lot thinking about you with your clients. I want you for myself and I know that won't be possible. I thought that you deserved an explanation in person rather than in a text message. I just wanted to say bye for the last time."

My face could not look away from his eyes, and each word he said struck me like a cold knife entering my stomach, but I didn't cry in front of him. I told him that I understood very well his feelings and that there was no other option but to finish. When we said goodbye and we cuddled by the tube station entrance, I remember feeling the earth disintegrating under my feet and eating me, deep inside the darkness. I walked inside the tube feeling the people walking pass me but my eyes were dead and looking nowhere. I was floating, nauseous and sweating, feeling my feet moving but I wasn't there.

That is the worst thing you can do to an escort. It took me a long time to recover from that.

Some people might ask how it's possible an escort can believe in love.

Well, many people won't accept a relationship with escorts however many of them would love sex with them. It would need a person that is mature, flexible, open minded and intelligent. This is a difficult task but not impossible. I know some escorts that do have steady relationships and they are happy but the truth is that many others struggle to get one because this.

CHAPTER 19

AL CAPONE 2003

After my boyfriend Anthony went back to his parent's house to sort out his bulimic problem I stayed in our flat on my own.

My life was very intense at the time, working full time as a manager in a Moroccan restaurant, studying part time at college to finish my access course just before going to University and trying to deal with Anthony serious problems.

It seemed that life wanted to test me as things became even worse.

The owner of the chain I was working for was an Iranian in his late forties and by calling him 'Al Capone the mafia boss' I was doing him a favour. I remember I accepted that job to try to step up the job ladder during my last year before going to university. Mr Fared made me a substantial offer to manage one of his restaurants. Apparently the previous manager was crap and made little profit so he needed someone fresh and full of energy with new ideas.

In exchange for a particularly suitable work schedule which was compatible with my studies and much better wages, I agreed to turn the restaurant around, train the staff and bring customers back to the business.

I was handed a very dirty restaurant, unmotivated and untrained staff, a dreary menu that had not changed for a year and few customers. I had a big challenge in front of me. Perfect.

For me a restaurant is not much different from a theatre play. You have the waiters who are the actors, the chefs are the hidden orchestra, the manager is the theatre director and don't forget the customers who are your audience.

After observing the restaurant dynamics and working methods, I organised a meeting of where I addressed the whole team.

"The restaurant is a disaster right now, but I can tell you, all of this is not your fault" I said to the staff. "Your previous manager has put the restaurant in this position but I have the solution to the problem. How much do you earn a week in tips?"

"About £10 or £20 per week, per head, Sir" said one of the two waiters-

"Well, in my previous job we were getting £120 tips a week."

Their eyes suddenly opened and I got their attention. "If you follow my advice and strict training during the next few weeks I can guarantee you all tips of around £60 per week in three months time, £90 tips in six months and gradual increases after that. But listen, I will be very tough and hard on all of you so be prepare to sweat."

"Are we all in the same boat?" I asked.

"Yes Pablo" Said all the staff, nodding their heads and smiling.

The first weeks were hard for us all as I was trying to put things right and break the bad habits the previous manger allowed.

This was achieved by cleaning the restaurant from floor to ceiling, retraining the waiters, changing the menus, creating a new atmosphere, advertising a new opening and bringing the customers back.

After three months the staff were getting £60 each in tips a week as promised, and that helped to motivate them and push them further so we could fill the restaurant to the maximum and double tables each night.

After five months we had queues of people outside the restaurant and the money was flowing like crazy.

The intensity of the work made the weeks pass quickly and the Head Office and Mr Farad's flattering comments blinded me about the kind of company I was dealing with.

The wages of the employees were delivered to each restaurant every month by head office staff in individual envelopes. Yes, a very unusual way of payment but we all had contracts and national insurance paid so we did not get suspicious until one day I was called to collect the wages at the Head Office myself.

When I arrived Mr Fared invited me in to his office. Two sexy secretaries (that I later learnt were his mistresses) were counting thousands of £20 notes. I was amazed when I saw such huge amount of cash all in one place. They went through the employee's hourly sheets and put the right amount in each envelope. While all that was happening Mr Fared held by my shoulders and we walked around the room.

"So Pablo, I heard that you are doing great with the new restaurant and that the staff are very happy." said Mr Fared, "But I also heard that you are getting lots of tips now."

"Yes Mr Fared, that is right" I said.

"Well I am the owner of that restaurant so I am entitled to 10% of the tips. From now on I want you to split off my part and send it to head office each month."

"But Mr Fared, the tips are the incentive to motivate the staff to work harder. That way they will be more efficient and make more money for you. With all respects, I don't think it is fair for you to take any percentage of the tips which customers leave for your staff and their hard work."

"With all respects to you Pablo, I think you are forgetting who the boss here is, don't you? There is no more discussion to be had. You will do as you are told. Now take the wages and take it to the staff."

When I left the office I was furious. I could not believe the boss wanted to steal his employee's tips. I took my phone and arranged an appointment with the Citizens Advice Bureau. They informed me that it is very unusual for companies to retain a percentage of the tips, however, they are allowed by the law to keep ten percent of any credit card tips.

I spoke with the staff and explained the situation. I would take ten percent from the credit card tips for head office but I wouldn't give one penny to them from the cash tips. Fortunately for us the head office could not know how much money we were getting in cash tips unless any of the staff told them. I asked them to keep it secret. They understood and agreed so they could have more tips for their hard work.

Two weeks afterwards one of the secretaries came to the restaurant. She was always very friendly with me. She came to warn me that Mr Fared, AKA Al Capone, was aware of the cash tips and he demanded the ten percent as ordered. She advised me not to confront him and just do what he wanted to avoid any problem.

I explained to her this wouldn't be possible as I promised the staff good tips in exchange for their hard work. By giving head office both cash and credit card tips I would be breaking my promises and lose the trust of all my staff.

"Is this your last word?" asked his mistress

"Yes, I will give a percentage of the credit card tips but not one penny from the cash tips, sorry."

Five days later a letter came from head office asking me to relocate to a different restaurant. They knew I wouldn't accept a move to that restaurant as it was the worst in the chain and far away from where I lived. Mr Al Capone was trying to humiliate me and put me between a rock and a hard place.

I had worked for the company for ten months already and my contract would expire in two months time just before I had to go to University. Mr Al Capone wanted to punish me for protecting my staff and not giving him what he wanted, so I had no other alternative.

"I have gathered all of you to let you know that I won't work in this restaurant anymore. Mr Fared wants me to do something that is not fair for any of you, I'll say even immoral. I am leaving the restaurant's keys and all the papers related to the company to you. It has been an enormous pleasure working with you all. Good bye" I said to all their shocked faces.

The news spread fast and I could imagine Mr Fared's angry face when getting the news. Pablo, the Spanish manager, left with his head held high without allowing himself to be humiliated.

With all this happening I totally forgot that I had borrowed a huge twenty inch modern HD Toshiba TV from the restaurant for the exhibition of my last project at college. I had asked for Mr Fared's permission to borrow the TV a month previously when things were fine. I invariably refused any of his treats, such as taking his Mercedes for a weekend or staying at one of his luxury properties for free so he happily gave me permission to borrow the TV. I arrived in the restaurant one day when it was closed to the public and told the chef that Mr Fared had agreed to lend me the TV from the top floor flat. He nodded and I took the TV while he was at work in the kitchen. He did not actually see me take the TV.

After I quit the restaurant my exams and presentations started straight away so I didn't have time to think about this issue, only to concentrate on my studies. Just after I finished my exams I got a call on my mobile.

"Is this Mr Pablo Gonzalez?" a serious male voice asked.

"Yes speaking, who is this?" I asked nervously.

"This is the police" the man said, "We've had a complaint from Mr Fared. He stated an item was stolen from his premises while you were working there and we would like you to come to our police station to ask you some questions.

I was shaken. I could not believe that he was playing such low game after all I had done for his restaurant.

"Yes Sir, I don't have anything to hide and actually have a lot to say about what kind of a man Mr Fared is. I will be happy to meet you and answer any questions" I replied.

The following day I took a folder with all the documents proving how much money the restaurant was making since I took over, the numbers about the tips, the letter with advice from the Citizens Advice Bureau and some other recommendation letters proving I was a trustworthy and good employee.

I was somewhat nervous as I had never been to a police station before to be questioned. On arrival a friendly policeman asked me to follow him. We went to a room with a long desk and I was told that I was there for interrogation. I could not believe what was happening.

"Mr Pablo Gonzales. We are now arresting you under suspicion of stealing private property from Mr Fared's premises. Please empty your pockets and leave all your items on the table" said the policeman while a policewoman was taking notes on her computer and asking me my personal details.

I was taken to a cell and left there for forty minutes. The cell was very small with a toilet, a wash basin and a place to rest with a mat near a window with bars.

Forty minutes later the door opened and the same policeman told me I was allowed to make a call. He took me to a private room with a desk and a phone on it.

"You have 10 minutes Mr Gonzales" said the policeman while closing the door.

On the desk were some documents with phone numbers, including legal aid. I called a lawyer and explained the situation to him. I was nervous and angry at that point.

"Mr Gonzales, from what I heard your situation is very simple" said the lawyer. "You haven't committed any crime at all and all this is just a misunderstanding. You just have to explain your story to the police and they will realise that you did nothing wrong."

His words made me more comfortable and I thanked him for his advice.

The policeman was waiting for me and we went to one of the interviews rooms. Before we started he explained to me what was about to happen.

"Mr Gonzales. I am about to start the interrogation and will ask you several questions. You can decide to remain silence or not. Everything will be recorded on tapes."

He showed me the five tapes and a huge recording machine where he started to insert each tape.

I was amazed by the situation. They were treating me like a high profile terrorist! But the words from the lawyer came back to me so I tried to relax and let him do his job.

He sat in front of me and asked me for my version of events. I took my folder with the documents and explained to him everything had happened from the beginning – how I was asked to take over the restaurant, made so much money for the owner in a short time, the owner's unconventional way of paying his employees with cash, his peculiar way of manipulating his managers by giving them extra treats on the side, and how I was forced to leave my job or be humiliated had I not accepted his decision of giving part of the tips to him.

I could see the policeman was surprised with my story and he was nodding and being sympathetic while listening.

"Mr Gonzales, do you have in your possession Mr Fared television?" he enquired. "We met Mr Fared at the restaurant and the Chef told us that he personally saw you taking the TV away."

"Yes I have. But the television was borrowed, not stolen, with the direct permission of Mr Fared. I asked Mr Fared to borrow the TV for a short period to be used in my final college project and he agreed. Just weeks after the tips problem unfolded, my exams started and I totally forgot about it" I explained.

I was hurt to discover that the chef had lied to the police and said that he personally saw me taking the TV. I realised then that Mr Al Capone threatened him with losing his job if he did not say that to the police.

"Well I think I have heard enough for now. As far as I am concerned no crime was committed here and the solution is very easy. You just have to give back the television to Mr Fared. Please follow me."

I was taken to the same reception room where I had been arrested and the policewoman gave me back my belongings. The policeman suggested that I returned the TV as soon as possible making sure that I got a receipt signed by them confirming the delivery.

"By the way, what does the TV look like? Is it just a small standard TV?" asked the policeman out of curiosity.

I was pleased to hear that question. For a moment I could not breathe and everything stopped in front of me.

So they don't have a clue what type of TV I borrowed? Al Capone was not able to give a description of the TV as he didn't have a receipt of purchase and he just mentioned a TV. The chef never saw the TV in person or me physically taking it so he just mentioned a TV without giving specifications.

"That's right" I said to the policeman, "It's actually a very old and small ten inch TV from the 80s that shows black and white images only. I'll return it as soon as possible and will come back to the station with the signed receipt conforming that I gave it back to them."

When I went back home, I stood in the middle of my lounge where I had the huge twenty inch TV and a very small TV which I had never used before. I couldn't help but smile when thinking about what I was about to do.

I called the restaurant at midday to confirm that the chef was there making the preparations for dinner while the restaurant was closed. He answered the phone but I didn't speak, I knew for sure that he was there now.

I called a taxi and took the old TV and a letter stating that the borrowed TV was delivered and returned by me, for the chef to sign.

When the chef opened the restaurant door and saw me carrying the TV in my hands he couldn't help but show horror on his face. He probably thought I was about to punch him after what he did. I was really enjoying the situation but I was nervous too.

"Hi, I am coming to return the famous TV" I said to the chef.

"If you don't mind I need to check that the TV is working properly before you go" he said in a trembling voice without looking into my eyes.

"Of course, feel free to do so!" I smiled.

After he checked the TV was working fine, I asked him to sign the letter confirming that I had returned the TV to the premises. I let out a brief smirk while he was signing. The same person who falsely stated he saw me taking the TV was now confirming that I had returned it. Of course he had no idea what kind of TV it was, so he thought it must be the TV I had taken in the first place.

I left the restaurant and walked away slowly while beaming and enjoying the victory.

I went back to the police and showed them the signed receipt. They made a copy of it.

To put the cherry on top of the cake I called one of the company staff with the excuse of saying good bye as I was leaving to go to university soon. This person was the typical type of employee you find in all companies, anything you say to them will be known two hours later by the rest of the staff.

I emphasised to her what Al Capone did to me and how he forced the chef to lie about me, my detention and how I switched the television at the last minute, giving back an old and crap TV instead.

I knew that hours later Mr Fared would be humiliated and the gossip would get all around the company. Everyone would enjoy the story and the way I took revenge on him.

My mission was accomplished and since then, every time I look at my nice big TV I remember that moment and my victory with a smile on the face.

CHAPTER 20

POPPERS MADNESS

For those who do not know what poppers are, they are a chemical liquid substance commonly known as 'alkyl nitrite'. Nitrites dilate blood vessels and allow more blood to get to the heart. Gay and straight people use it during sex to get high or a fast head rush by inhaling its scent. The substance is legal in the UK and you can buy it in sex shops or even online.

I rarely take any drugs during sex but I love poppers and my clients do too, therefore I have to be stocked with them all the time. The poppers are good fun but when abused can create some serious problem and reactions:

Chemical burns to body tissues – with the development of a rash around the nose and mouth, and/or irritation of the nose and throat.

Feelings of sickness, faintness and weakness.

Death if swallowed; or if used by individuals with heart problems.

I will never forget one when day I met a client on an out call. He worked in finance at Canary Wharf and had a modern apartment with river views. He was in his middle forties, a bit overweight (probably based on his sedentary life at a desk) and he was very friendly.

We had a nice glass of red French wine and a chat first. Then we went to the bedroom. He was into domination and rough play so I asked him to kneel on the floor and start licking my feet. While I was playing with him he was taking poppers constantly. He was getting very excited and high.

While he was on the bed on all fours he had his head down and the poppers to his nose, he shouted "fuck me, fuck me!" I started to pound him and flog him at the same time when suddenly I noticed that his whole body crumbled like a puppet. Something was wrong. I stopped immediately and started to shake him gently. His face and hands were pure purple in colour.

I asked him to breathe deeply and after two minutes he started to recover and said he needed to go to the bathroom. I helped him to walk, holding his arm, but when we arrived in the walk-in shower he suddenly fainted and fell to the floor.

I was worried. His eyes were looking to the front, still, and I could not feel his breath. He was having a blackout and I could feel my heart beat quickening. I started to call his name and slap his face while shouting at him.

"Try to breathe, breathe deeply!" I said.

So many images flashed through my head during those minutes; the porter of the building showing the police my signature in the guest book, the ambulance arriving and doing first aid on my client and me explaining to the police what had happened. I needed to calm down and try to help him. I could not just leave it there and go.

I opened the shower and splashed some water on his face, slapped him again while asking him to breath. I noticed that his eyes moved and he started to breathe again.

Thank god, he is coming back, I thought.

I stayed with him on the floor holding his face and body while he recovered and started to breathe regularly. I asked him to stay down for five minutes until his blood pressure recovered and the purple colour started to fade.

When he was ok again he went to the lounge and sat on the sofa. He poured another glass of wine and started drinking.

"You are a lovely guy Pedro" he said.

He was acting like nothing had happened. I had the impression this was not the first time he had blacked out. He clearly had blood pressure problems and a weak heart, and the excess of poppers made him faint. He was aware of that but he did not care.

I was very upset as he nearly died in front of me but I was not there to judge him or patronise him so I decided not to make a fuss.

"One day you will be with a less considerate escort that might panic and will leave you there. That will be your last time of pleasure, so be careful" I said.

He smiled and nodded his head.

☧ ☧ ☧

My second poppers madness was during an in-call at my place. I was with a young client, nineteen years old. He was a handsome Muslim Indian and wanted to have his first full sexual experience in a discreet way with a guy he fancied. He decided to contact me and arranged a meeting. He was very nervous when he arrived but I explained to him that he was in good hands and that I would do my best to make sure he had a good time. I suggested we start with a sensual massage to warm up and go from there.

After the massage we started kissing and playing around. I asked him if he wanted to get fucked and he answered he wanted to try everything that day. While I was putting on a condom I asked him if he wanted to take poppers, thinking that would help him to relax and have a more intense experience. He said yes and I passed him the bottle. I was finishing putting the condom on when I realised that he was pouring the bottle in his mouth.

"What the hell are you doing? Are you crazy!" I shouted.

It was a too late; he had already swallowed the whole bottle. I knew that nitrates can burn the skin and human tissue quickly so I jumped out of the bed and ran to the kitchen to get a full pint of milk. When I went back to the room I asked him how he was feeling, he said he was feeling sick and very hot. I insisted he drank the milk straight away to neutralise the acid.

After drinking the whole pint he went to the toilet and started to vomit. Then he lay on the bed and I asked him to relax. I was distraught.

"Why did you drink the poppers?"

"You asked me if I wanted to take some poppers so I thought I had to drink it. I have never done that before" he answered.

"I am sorry but you cannot drink the poppers, you have to inhale them through your nose. I thought you knew that. I didn't have time to react as you drank the bottle straight away in one second. Well, you know now. If you feel sick after leaving my place you should go to the hospital straight away and let me know."

"I'm feeling better already, don't worry."

I thought I would never see him again after such a crazy experience but he called again several weeks later and we had a great session, this time without poppers.

Poppers are like everything else in life, all things in moderation.

I had great times during sex when taking poppers; they bring me to a different sexual level. Pedro only takes them some times as he likes to be in control, but Pablo gets crazy with them as he likes to lose control and fly during sex.

CHAPTER 21

THE ADVENTURE 2007

After I finished my degree most of my University friends took a break for travelling, going on adventures or just relaxing before entering real life and starting a job.

I knew it would be a waste of time to stay longer in that little town which had hosted me for three years during my degree. I had to move to London for a brighter future. My plan instead of travelling was to spend four months enjoying London life and then to settle down in the big city before I started to look seriously for a job. Once I found a nice house in London I continued doing escorting to pay my bills.

During my degree and living in such little town I didn't have another option but to concentrate on my studies and work hard to pay for my living costs there. I even started escorting in my last year to be able to pay for my final project at University. I didn't want to ask for help from my family. I achieved all that on my own but I had no personal life. I was craving adventure and wild sex.

During my first months in London I concentrated on organising my house, settling down, visiting places and meeting sexy guys. I also decided to enjoy 'la vida loca', by that I mean lots and lots of sex!

One of my fuck buddy's in London was a black guy called Kevin, contacted me online for a meet. I told him that I had a sexual fantasy that I would like to fulfil.

"Please tell me" he insisted

"I would like to meet a group of black guys, all tops and with XXL tools. I want them to gang bang me one after the other."

"I see, well I have a group of black friends who are very well endowed that I am sure will enjoy meeting a gorgeous Spanish boy like you. How many guys do you want?"

"I think six guys would be perfect. Could you organise that for me?"

"Done!" Kevin said.

When I arrived at his house for the gang bang I was very nervous and excited. The guys were sitting in the lounge wearing casual clothes. They were in their late twenties and some in their early thirties, all of them masculine, tall and fit. We had a bit of a chit-chat and suddenly one of them asked me from the sofa to take my clothes off. I was a bit intimidated by the situation but I obeyed.

"Get closer to me, on your knees" said one of them.

He started to kiss me while I was on my knees and another one started to touch my body and my ass from behind. He undid his trousers and indicated to me to suck him off.

The other guys were already taking off their clothes and I noticed that all of them were extremely well hung. There was nothing under nine inches in that room.

Everything went very fast and intense from there. They took turns to play with me, and believe me they were not gentle once the game started. I could feel my ass being pounded hard in all the positions imaginable. They moved me from one place to another in the room and fucked me like animals.

For first time in my life I tried double penetration. I sat on one of them while he was lying on the floor. Once his ten inch tool was pounding me from under another one approached me from behind and slowly inserted his cock too. The feeling was astounding. I started moaning like crazy while they were pushing hard and deep inside me.

The session lasted three hours, not stopping even for a minute. When we finished one of them approached me to shake hands.

"We didn't think that you would be able to take it all. We are amazed. You did very well!" he said.

I smiled with satisfaction but it didn't last long as when I tried to walk home my ass burned like crazy. I would say that the pain I had during the next two days was worthwhile. I finally felt like one of the girls I saw in my brothers' porn magazines years ago.

One week later I decided to experiment with my dark side and meet a master dominant top. I chatted online with a guy into kinky stuff, a dom top in his late thirties from Greece who was visiting London. I explained to him that I was looking for an aggressive top in bed and that I wanted to lose control, being used hard in an intense session.

He requested meeting in public one evening for a drink first. I normally don't do that but I accepted.

He was a very attractive guy, super fit, masculine and with stubble. I could not take my eyes off his big greenish-blue eyes. He had a mysterious aura and spoke calmly like he was fully in control, but at the same time friendly.

He proposed to go for a walk. We started to move away from the main streets, he was directing the walk. We entered a small semi-dark alley and suddenly he stopped walking. I turned and looked at him.

"Open your trousers and pull them down slightly" he demanded.

I was nervous and confused. I looked to the right and the left to check if anyone was coming. He was looking at me in a very firm way. I pulled my trousers down to my knees slowly. He approached me and pushed me against a walk, and then he turned me around putting my face against the wall.

I could hear my heart beating fast and I was getting extremely excited. He started to touch me and grabbed my balls with one hand, pulling them down slowly. I objected but he did not stop.

He spit on his other hand and started to play with my ass, fingering me while he continuing to pull my balls harder with the other hand. He was licking my neck and breathing into my ear.

"You like it, don't you little cunt?" he whispered in my ear.

I had a huge hard on. He suddenly stopped and asked me to put my clothes on again.

Later I understood that this was his way to test me and check how much I was willing to comply and follow orders.

"Let's go to my apartment" he said. "It is nearby."

When we arrived he was calmly and didn't speak for a while so I decided to sit on a sofa in the lounge in silence. By this time he was pouring a glass of red wine while looking at me.

"Undress and stand in the middle of the room" he instructed.

He brought a blindfold and put it on me. He didn't speak for at least two minutes but I could hear him walking around me slowly and the sound of him taking his belt off.

He commenced to beat my body hard, on my legs, on my back, on my arms and so on. I complained of the pain but I didn't move from my place. Silence again.

"Come here" he ordered from another part of the room. "Get on your knees and come to me.

I tried to discover where he was by following the sound of his voice, and when I arrived I felt the heat of his body on my skin.

He pushed my face to the floor with one hand and asked me to lick his feet.

"Go up slowly, lick my leg."

He opened a bottle of poppers and asked me to sniff deep.

When I went up his leg and approached his genital area I was very high on poppers.

"Lick my underwear."

Suddenly he took his cock out and forced me to suck it, pushing my face down with both hands.

"Take more poppers" he ordered.

He then pushed me back, and standing in front of me he started to force fuck my face while using the belt to beat me when he was not happy with my actions.

"Take more poppers."

Then he pushed me violently to the floor and started to kick my legs and body while I took the foetal position to protect myself.

"Get on your fours, you cunt."

He put a condom on and started to fuck me without any lube, just some saliva.

Again he ordered "Take more poppers."

Then while fucking me aggressively he started to punch my back and butt hard. I was flying. All that was new for me but I was enjoying being forced and punished for the pleasure I was getting.

"Take more poppers now, cunt."

He put his belt around my neck and held me like a dog while I was on my fours, pulling the lead and forcing me to walk. He took me to the toilet and pushed my head inside the basin.

"Take more poppers, cunt, but keep you face inside the toilet" he growled.

He spread lube on my ass and his fingers started to push inside me. First two, then three, then four. Half of his hand was already inside me, sliding in and out.

"Take the poppers again cunt."

His five fingers started to push and I resisted.

"Relax your body and take poppers!" he barked.

His hand started to push slowly and before I could stop him he was already inside me. I could hear the echo of my heavy breathing inside the toilet basin and my heart beat going crazy.

He started to fist me, working his hand in and out of my ass.

The feeling was strange and overwhelming. He had full control of my body in that moment.

He took his hand out and stood over me with his legs on each side of my body. Suddenly I felt his piss pouring down my back, to my head and then into the toilet. When he finished he flushed the toilet with my head still inside.

He pulled the lead and forced me to walk back to the room where he sat on the sofa. He asked me to stay on my knees and watch him. He started to masturbate in front of me and I could see his thick eight inches getting hard. After a couple of minutes he came all over the floor. He was a heavy cummer and his milk went everywhere.

"You know what you have to do now" he said. "Lick every drop from the floor."

I will never forget that session. The guy was an expert in domination and brought me to a different sexual level, making me do things that I never thought I would do.

I had a lot of fun during that four month break and I learnt many things that I have used for Pedro since, this time Pedro being the Dom.

Having had my adventures I again started to apply for jobs while I continued doing escorting.

CHAPTER 22

THE HEDONISTIC CONSOLER

I guess at this point you are already asking yourself, why is this kind of guy doing escorting?

Well here are my reasons:

The first reason is practicality. I can earn more in one week than what I could earn in a month doing a basic normal job, so the money factor is quite motivational. That money helps me to survive in an expensive city like London and at the same time to save some money and finance my other projects.

The second reason is time. Doing this job I get many free hours per week that I can use on other things that are important to me, my projects, my other personal work, studies or anything I want. My schedule is much more flexible than doing a normal job.

The third reason is hedonism. Every satisfied client is like a caress to my ego. Every nice comment or admiration reinforces my hedonistic attitude. Clients unconsciously idealise escorts and create their own particular perception about your persona, which usually is far away from the real you.

Do you feel humiliated or used while doing escorting?

No I don't feel humiliated at all, however I am definitely used by my clients to fulfil their fantasies and basic needs. When I meet clients it's all about them, not about me. That is the reason I charge them.

Do you have a feeling of power when doing your job or do you feel dominated?

With my clients, I am the one in control most of the time. I like the way they look at me, I know they have chosen me and I know their expectations. I know they want me and need me at that moment to satisfy them. That is a powerful feeling.

What is the hardest thing for you?

Not being able to tell everyone what I do.

When you become an escort you separate yourself from the 'normal world'. Your job is totally unlike others; it doesn't follow the same rules. Suddenly your status has changed. You are doing something not many people would understand or accept, but at the same time you are admired by the people who need you to fulfil their basic cherished needs.

So is everything about sex? Sex is what brings people to me, but with time I have realised that escorting is not all about sex.

Most of my clients just want a person who won't judge them for their sexual tendencies or peculiar requests, they just want horny sex.

Other clients are looking for a different kind of encounter. They are not necessarily looking just for sexual relief but for warm human contact. On many occasions I have spent hours cuddling and kissing, listening to their stories without them demanding anything more. That showed me that for some, human contact was more important than the sexual part.

I have a regular client called Mark, who visits me every two months for a session. He is married to a woman and has two kids. Every time we meet he tells me the same story over and over. He is in love with a Brazilian heterosexual man in London. He helped the Brazilian to get a job, sorting out legal papers for him and even financially. Mark met his family and tried by all means to get closer to him but he never admitted his feelings for him. He described the Brazilian man's new girlfriend as a 'bitch' that is separating his beloved man from him. His obsession goes to a level that Mark even goes to visit him when his girlfriend is there. He goes to the toilet to see if he can find any used condoms. One day he found one full of cum so obviously the Brazilian guy had had sex with his girlfriend before he arrived. He took the condom and poured its content in his mouth.

"I finally could have a bit of him inside me" said Mark to me with a lascivious expression.

The Brazilian started to get annoyed with my client's persistency and intrusion so stopped calling him. Mark did not pick up on this and he continued to visit him and to knock on his door. The Brazilian reported him to the police as a stalker and then Mark's family discovered what was happening. He explained to me how he could not stop being in love with him and how he felt betrayed and humiliated in front of his family.

I have to listen the same story each time he comes to visit me and afterwards he invariably asks "What would you do in my case?"

I normally answer the same. "The Brazilian man has been taking advantage of you."

Just after that he always ask me to put my cock between his legs and he starts shouting "fuck my pussy with your big cock! Fuck my pussy like a Brazilian would do!"

When we finish he tells me how great I am and thanks me for listening.

"I can't speak about this subject with anyone else" he says.

Are escorts hedonistic consolers then? You decide.

CHAPTER 23

THE PITY 2008

I discovered through the years that the worst human disease is not Cancer or HIV, but self- pity. Self-pity is what causes wide spread depression today. This is ignited by the pressures of the modern society. A society of 'I want'; I want a good job, good clothes, a nice house, the perfect partner, the latest gadgets, a great perfect body that is never perfect enough, I want holidays, I want money, lots of it, recognition and success. I want, I want, I want. When we don't get this in the amount we wish, the self-pity appears, the dark days take over and we spiral downwards.

In one short month in 2008 self-pity brought me to darkness. Everything started to fail and go wrong; a negative cloud surrounded and covered me, each day more intensely. After my break of four months to settle and enjoy London, I spent six months applying for jobs related to my uni studies but had no positive responses. My escort job started to go wrong too and I didn't have many clients. On the top of that I got a serious bout of flu.

I could not understand what was going on, why was this happening to me? What had I done to deserve such bad luck and horrible troubles? The solution and answer was in front of me but I did not see it for a while.

I created that situation at the moment I stopped believing in myself. Self-pity invaded me without notice and took control. Everything started to go wrong then.

When I realised about the problem I took immediate action. It was like a personal battle against self-pity. I love challenges so it was perfect for me. I entered a war against this illness. I started to think positively, to write down all the good things I value about myself. I included things that I had achieved or done well, my positive aspects and strengths. Then I marked down projects and things to accomplish short term. I put them on my wall so every day I could see them and remind myself that I was in a battle and I could not let self-pity defeat me.

Everything started to run smoothly and I achieved all my short term goals fast.

I have the antidote now and I never let the self-pity reside in me again.

I have been fortunate in my life. If I died today I could proudly say that I have always done what I wanted when I wanted. I might not be rich, have a house or be married. These values and things are what most people think they should reach out for. But I am mortgage and debt free so I can choose where and how to be at any time. My life has been and will be driven by small challenges and once I achieve one, the next one is waiting. I chose, and my choices are things that make me happy or bring more knowledge.

To have small or big goals are crucial for me, but it's also important to be passionate and believe in them. Something magical happens when you concentrate on your goals and dreams.

You feel alive and things start happening around you that help accomplish your goals.

CHAPTER 24

AMEN

"Jesus said unto them: I tell you the truth, the tax collectors and the prostitutes are entering the kingdom of God ahead of you. For John came to you to show you the way of righteousness, and you did not believe him, but the tax collectors and the prostitutes did. And even after you saw this, you did not repent and believe him"

—Matthew 21:32

☧ ☧ ☧

I opened the door and I saw a man in his late fifties, quite tall and slim, wearing old fashioned humble clothes, with white short hair.

"Hi Pedro, I am Renoir" said my client with a French accent, smiling.

I took him to my room and I offered him a drink but he refused.

"Shall we start with a massage and go from there?" I asked as usual.

He nodded his head, started to take off his clothes, folded them carefully and left them on a chair, with the majestic precision of a ritual ceremony.

I was already naked on the bed. I asked him to lay down on his front and I started to massage his back while I sat on the top of him. I realised then that his spine was deformed and he had a prominent hump. His body was amorphous, very slim limbs with flaccid muscles, possibly from the lack of exercise and a large belly.

After the massage I asked him to turn around and started to frottage my body with his while kissing him.

"What do you want to do?" I whispered into his ear while moving on the top of him.

"Everything" he said.

He kept quiet during most of the session but when I started to fuck him he started to moan calmly, but he was trying to control himself and avoid making too much noise. Suddenly he started to whisper in another language. At the beginning I thought it was French but when I got closer to his head I realised he was speaking in Latin.

"Deus dimitte me. E frame est infirmitas" he whispered under his breath.

I was started to be more than a little intrigued about this client so when we finished I decided to stay on the bed and chat with him.

"I noticed that you were speaking in Latin" I said.

"Did you understand what I said?"

"No, but I studied Latin at school so I recognised the language."

"I am a priest" he said.

Silence invaded the room. We didn't speak for a couple of minutes.

"So I can see you like Richard Dawkins" he said, breaking the silence while pointing at one of my books on the shelf called 'The God Delusion'.

"I am afraid you have chosen an Atheist escort, Father" I said while smiling.

We chatted for a while. He confessed this was his first time with an escort. He decided to come to London for a short trip to do some shopping and meet me, and then he would go back to his parish in the south of France. While listening to his story I couldn't help but picture him doing a religious service at his church, preaching the bible while everyone paid attention.

It felt very weird to be in bed with a priest but the more he spoke the more I realised he was a good man. He was just human like the rest of us, including his flesh needs.

I didn't know him personally enough to judge him. But what I know for sure is that I prefer him to be a hypocrite and satisfy his needs with a male escort in a discreet way rather than abusing underage kids like some other priests do.

He visited me again months after, but this second time the conversation got a bit more inquisitive and he noticed that I was not comfortable with the fact that after having sex with me he was preaching the opposite values to his followers at church. We never met again after that.

☧ ☧ ☧

"Hi Pedro I am calling to enquire about your services. I wonder if you offer CP?" asked a client on the phone.

"Yes I play CP. What kind are you into?"

"I like canning. Do you have any canes?"

"Yes I have got two canes at my place. What else would you like to include in the session?"

"I am just looking for severe canning, nonstop, until I can't take any more."

When I opened my door I saw a Jewish guy with side curls smiling at me. My eyes were wide open.

"Hi, please come in" I said, trying to hide my surprise.

When he started to undress I noticed he was wearing very weird clothes like the ones I saw in the film "Yentl" starring Barbra Streisand.

After taking off many layers of attire he lay on my bed on his front and extended his arms to both sides in a cross position.

When I saw him in such a pose I couldn't help feeling that I was just about to cane a Jesus Christ look alike.

The spanking lasted twenty five minutes. My arm hurt but his ass was probably burning after the severe canning.

Each time I asked him if he wanted more, he replied yes, so I didn't pause during the punishment.

When we finished he started to dress calmly and kept looking at me while smiling.

Silence.

"Is everything ok?" I asked confusedly, while he kept smiling and looking.

"Yes, I am a Rabbi."

More silence.

"My service is fully discreet so you don't need to be worry about anything" I assured him.

"Thank you". He then paid me and left.

Perhaps you are starting to understand why I am an atheist now, aren't you?

CHAPTER 25

EXIT 2012

I have been a male escort for five years now and I do not regret it at all. I know I will have to exit at some point.

Escorting is like smoking however, it's difficult to stop.

The first client is always weird, like the first cigarette, but when you see the £100 in your hands for one hour's work, you get a buzz in the same way as nicotine is for smokers. That is the main honey trap.

Then with time you realise that escorting is a lifestyle that not many people would understand but not in fact much different from others. You become a sales man, but what you sell is your body, your understanding of people and your capacity to satisfy your clients in different ways.

Doing escorting can give you the freedom of being your own boss. You also enjoy the travelling, the money, the excitement of meeting interesting VIP people, learning about many new sexual options and activities, being perceived as a sex god by certain clients and the glamour of luxury hotels and special events.

However as all jobs, escorting has its downside too. There are sexual health risks, pressures to look good all the time, the high cost of advertisement and sex tools, the psychological ups and down, the double difficulty of having a real relationship while doing the job, being on call most the time and managing your personal time, judgments of bigoted people who don't accept or understand your job and the temptation of drugs.

The longer you do the job the more difficult it is to exit. You get used to a lifestyle and status somewhat different to other people and the money spoils you. But it is the gap in our normal careers when we finish escorting that becomes a real issue.

How can you justify a three or five year's gap in your CV when applying for a new job? "I was an escort and fucking very wealthy people for money". I don't think so.

I am not sure how much longer I will be an escort but I already have a plan B on the go.

In the meantime, Pedro and Pablo can still coexist doing their best and having fun.

My phone is ringing.

Would you excuse me for a moment?

"Hello?"

"Is this Pedro?"

"Yes, Pedro speaking."

"Hi Pedro, are you available today?

"Yes, I am around. What type of session are you looking for?" Pedro says with a naughty smile...

TERMINOLOGY

Anal beads – A string of beads inserted into the anus and often pulled out during orgasm.

Anorgasmic – Incapable of having an orgasm.

Autofellatio – For a man to perform oral sex on himself, putting his penis in his own mouth.

Autoerotic strangulation – Suffocating oneself via strangulation for sexual stimulation, especially to increase the intensity of orgasm. A dangerous practice that sometimes results in death.

Bareback (BB) – Having sex without a condom, especially for anal sex.

BDSM – *abbr.* Short for 'Bondage and Discipline, Sadism and Masochism.' A catch-all term for a broad array of sexual practices, especially involving restraint and inflicting pain.

Bestiality – Sexual interest or sexual acts with animals; Zoophilia.

Bloodsports – BDSM play that involves blood, including cutting and piercing.

Bottom – The receiver, who is penetrated. The submissive person in BDSM activity. Opposite of top.

Breath play or control – Restricting airflow, by strangulation, suffocation, or other means for sexual stimulation.

Bukkake – When many men ejaculate on the face of a man or a woman. Also called facial.

Butt plug – A sex toy designed for anal penetration that has a flared base. Usually smaller than a typical dildo and not shaped like a penis.

CBT – Cock and balls torture. By pulling or punching or pinching or spanking the genital male parts to create sexual pleasure through pain.

Chastity – The use of chastity devices on men or woman to avoid that person having sexual climax. The key holder takes control and they decide when the other person will be released and allowed to have an orgasm. These devices can be used by couples to stimulate their sexual life.

Cock ring – A device, often a leather strap, placed at the base of an erect penis in order to restrict blood flow and maintain an erection.

Come (cum) – Semen. Also spelled 'cum'. Or to cum (come) meaning to ejaculate or having an orgasm.

Coprophagia (scat) – Eating faeces (shit). It is considered a dangerous sexual practice. Also called scat play.

Cottaging – Is a British gay slang term referring to anonymous sex between men in a public lavatory.

CP –Corporal punishment. By spanking with flog, cane, paddle or belt. By punching, kicking or giving corporal punishment to create sexual pleasure.

Cross-dress – For a man to wear women's clothing. Used especially for men who only occasionally dress as women but maintain their masculine identity.

Crushing – A fetish practice where someone steps on food, insects, or even small animals.

Cut – Circumcised. Opposite of uncut.

Dildo – A cylindrical sex toy, often shaped like a penis, used to penetrate the vagina or anus. Usage note: A dildo generally refers to a toy with no moving parts, as opposed to a vibrator which includes an electric motor and vibrates.

Deep throat – Fellatio in which the penis is inserted far into the mouth, entering the throat.

Dipping – To partially insert the top of the penis in the vagina or anus several times, teasing it but without performing full penetration.

Dirty Sanchez – Performing oral sex on someone after they engage in anal sex. After anal sex, wiping off the dirty penis or hand on the person's upper lip, to simulate a moustache.

Doggie style – Sexual intercourse where the man enters the woman or man by her / his back side; also called rear-entry.

Dominator (or dominatrix) – The dominant person in a bondage or S&M relationship. Dom for male and dominatrix for female.

Domination – Type of role play where one person takes the role of dominant controlling the submissive. This kind of role play can be mild but at times quite aggressive and tough depending on the level agreed to play.

Donkey punch – Having anal sex with someone and punching them in the back of the head to make them pass out. Said to induce a clenching of the anal sphincter in the unconscious person.

Douche – The action of cleaning the vagina or the rectum by using an enema or douche nozzle adapted to fix into the shower hose.

Down low – Slang term that refers to a subculture of men who usually identify as heterosexual, but who have sex with men; some avoid sharing this information even if they have female sexual partner(s) The term is also used to refer to a related sexual identity. *'The Down Low is a lifestyle predominately practiced by young, urban African American men who have sex with other men and women, yet do not identify as gay or bisexual.*

DP – Double penetration. Could be performed by two men or one man using his penis and one sex toy at the same time.

Edge play – Potentially dangerous sexual practices, often involving pain. Another absent bit of advice I wish I would have seen is in regard to fireplay (the practice usually includes acts of setting someone's partner on fire in controlled ways that usually leave no burns). This type of edge play is particularly edgy for larger people if their partner allows alcohol to pool in the folds of their skin.

Electro – The use of sex electrical machines are common in S&M play and is used to stimulate sexually the other person or for punishment. Some machines include pads that can be located in different parts of the body to make certain muscles contract. Others include a wand that gives small electric shocks when in contact with the body.

Facesitting – A fetish practice where a woman sits on a man's face or a man sits on a man's face, forcing her or him to rim and perform anal oral sex.

Felch – To ejaculate into an anus and then lick or suck the semen out. Also asking the receiver to push the semen out and making him /her to drink it.

Feet worship – Foot fetishism, foot worship, or podophilia is a pronounced sexual interest in feet. Foot fetishism has been defined as a pronounced sexual interest in the feet or footwear. It is a mainly male interest.

Fetish – A strong sexual interest in or obsession over some object, body part, or activity. Examples include foot fetish, latex fetish cum fetish, leather, body smells, piss, food, the list is endless. Also used broadly to describe any non-traditional sex, especially BDSM.

Fisting – To place much of the hand, or the entire hand, in the vagina or anus. Some including the whole arm.

Flogging – Beating with a whip, strap or rope as a form of punishment.

Foot job – Rubbing feet on the penis, usually until ejaculation.

Frottage – Rubbing against someone else for sexual pleasure without engaging in penetration.

Gang bang – When many men have sex with a single woman or man, one after another or even at the same time.

Glory hole – A hole cut through a wall or door, allowing anonymous sex between people on either side of the wall. Often found in gay sex clubs.

Go down – To perform oral sex on a man or woman. 'I went down on him'.

Golden shower – Urinating on someone else. Also called 'water sports'.

Head (giving head) – Oral sex, specifically performed on a man.

Infantilism (nappies play) – A fetish practice where an adult role-plays being an infant, wearing baby clothing and sometimes being disciplined by a mother figure. Also called 'nappies play'.

Kinky – Sexual activity that is somehow non-traditional or exotic.

Lubricant (lube) – A slippery substance used to make sex more comfortable and pleasurable.

Ménage a trois – When three people have sex together at once. A threesome.

Mummification – BDSM bondage practice involves restraining a living person's body in a non-damaging way by wrapping it head to toe, or neck to toe, in materials like saran wrap, cling film, cloth, bandages, rubber strips, duct tape, plaster bandages, body bags, or straitjackets.

The end result is a person completely immobilized and looking like an Egyptian mummy. They may then either be left bound in a state of effective sensory deprivation for a period of time, or sensually stimulated in their state of bondage, before being released from their wrappings.

Mummification is often used to enhance a feeling of total bodily helplessness, and incorporated with sensation play.

Necrophilia – The desire to have sex with dead people.

Nooner – A sexual encounter during the lunchtime hour, especially one that takes place at the office.

Orgasm – The pleasurable, climactic release of sexual tension. In a man, it is usually accompanied by ejaculation.

Orgy – A sexual encounter with three or more people. Group sex.

Paraphilia – A sexual obsession, usually over an object or sex act.

A Paraphilia refers to a form of sexual gratification that is based on use of a particular object, technique, or situation, usually to the exclusion of other avenues of sexual fulfilment. Examples include frotteurism (sexual arousal is achieved by rubbing up against people) and various forms of cross-dressing or transvestism.

Peg – To use a strap-on dildo on someone. 'My girlfriend loves to peg me because she enjoys the power trip'.

Polyamory – Having sexual relationships with more than one person.

'Polyamory' comes from the Greek word for 'multiple' and the Latin word for 'love.' We use it to refer to amorous relationships which deliberately and openly involve more than two partners.

Poppers – Poppers are a common slang term for a range of chemical psychoactive drugs called alkyl nitrites (in particular, the inhalant drug amyl nitrite). Initially, the term came into use in the 1960s, when amyl nitrite, then used as a heart medicine, was sold in capsules that were cracked, or "popped," to release the chemical.

Although rarely used for heart problems today, amyl nitrite is still used to treat cyanide poisoning. Poppers are widely used as recreational drugs, especially on the gay scene, and are typically taken as fumes inhaled directly from small bottles. Poppers are cheap and easy to acquire, often sold as room deodorizer or as sex enhancers in sex shops, although their use carries significant risks. Amyl nitrite was first synthesized in 1844 by Antoine Jérôme Balard and was popularized as a treatment for angina pectoris by Sir Thomas Lauder Brunton. However, it only became recognized as a recreational drug in the 1960s, initially in the gay community. Gay men discovered that poppers helped them feel relaxed mentally and physically, increased sexual arousal, made anal sex easier and less painful, and enhanced orgasm.

Pre-cum – A small amount of clear fluid sometimes emitted by the penis during sexual arousal/stimulation but before ejaculation.

Priapism – A medical condition characterized by a painful erection that won't go down.

Pumping – Sometimes euphemistically called male enhancement, are techniques alleged to increase the girth, length, or hardness of the human penis. A penis pump is a cylinder that is fitted over the penis, with a manual or motorized pump to create suction. The apparatus creates a partial vacuum around the penis, engorging it as blood is drawn in. As vacuum increases, the difference between the inner blood pressure and the pump pressure increases as well; excessive vacuum causes vascular damage.

Penis pumps can be used to temporarily overcome symptoms of impotence, but do not cure the condition: a ring must be applied to maintain the erection which will otherwise immediately subside. Pumps may work even if there is nerve or vascular damage preventing a natural erection.

Quickie – Sexual intercourse that is short in duration.

Rainbow sex – Performing oral sex on a woman while she is menstruating.

Rimming – Performing oral sex on the anus, especially licking the edge of the anus.

Raw – Sex without a condom.

Rusty trombone – When someone licks a man's ass and reaches around to the front to masturbate his penis. So called because it appears that the person is blowing into the ass and manipulating the penis like a musical instrument. Also may refer to performing oral sex on a man right after he's engaged in anal sex.

Sleaze sex – Sex which crosses the line, it would pick up such nickname as "radical," "pornographic," "underground" or "XXX."

Sounding – Urethral play can involve the introduction of either soft or rigid items into the penis (as well as further in). Objects such as sounds are usually only inserted about halfway into the glands and can usually be easily retrieved. Other toys and items, such as catheters, may be introduced deeper; in some cases even into the bladder. Some items may even be allowed to curl several times or expand within the bladder. This action in the male may be directly or indirectly associated with stimulation of the prostate gland and some types of bladder control.

Stomp – The act of throwing someone on the ground and stepping on them very hard over and over again to create sexual pleasure and pain.

Tea room – A public toilet where gay men often have sex.

Teabagging – When a man lowers his testicles down onto someone's mouth. So-called because of the resemblance to lowering a teabag into water.

Tease – To cause arousal in someone or the expectation of sexual activity without following through on that promise.

Tina (Crystal Meth) – Methamphetamine is a white crystalline drug that people take by snorting it (inhaling through the nose), smoking it or injecting it with a needle. Some even take it orally, but all develop a strong desire to continue using it because the drug creates a false sense of happiness and well-being—a rush (strong feeling) of confidence, hyperactiveness and energy. One also experiences decreased appetite. These drug effects generally last from six to eight hours, but can last up to twenty-four hours.

The first experience might involve some pleasure, but from the start, methamphetamine begins to destroy the user's life.

Crystal meth is used by individuals of all ages, but is most commonly used as a "club drug," taken while partying in night clubs or at rave parties. Its most common street names are *ice* or *glass*.

It is a dangerous and potent chemical and, as with all drugs, a poison that first acts as a stimulant but then begins to systematically destroy the body. Thus it is associated with serious health conditions, including memory loss, aggression, psychotic behaviour and potential heart and brain damage.

Highly addictive, meth burns up the body's resources, creating a devastating dependence that can only be relieved by taking more of the drug.

Top – The giver. The dominant person in BDSM activity.

TT – *abbr.* Tits torture. By pinching the nipples with the fingers or nails or using pegs or vacuums pumps, needles, etc.

Vanilla – Non-kinky, 'traditional' sex.

Waxing – BDSM game where hot wax is poured on the submissive person's body to create pain and sexual pleasure.

3895502R00099

Printed in Great Britain
by Amazon.co.uk, Ltd.,
Marston Gate.